¡ViVA DESSERTS!

Traditional & Reinvented Sweets *from a* Mexican-American Kitchen

NICOLE PRESLEY

Published by Familius LLC, www.familius.com
PO Box 1249 Reedley, Ca 93654.

Familius books are available at special discounts for bulk purchases,
whether for sales promotions or for family or corporate use.
For more information, contact Familius Sales at orders@familius.com.

Library of Congress Control Number: 2022934975

Print ISBN 978-1-64170-735-0
Ebook ISBN 978-1-64170-766-4
KF 978-1-64170-776-3
FE 978-1-64170-786-2

Printed in China

Photos taken by Mando Lopez
Author photo taken by Luz Gallardo
Edited by Ashlin Awerkamp, Peg Sandkam, and Sarah Echard
Cover and book design Brooke Jorden

10 9 8 7 6 5 4 3 2 1

First Edition

This book is dedicated to the loves of my life,
my three Ms: Mando, Max, and Mom.

Contents

Mexican-American Fusion Desserts: These recipes intertwine both my cultures. They are American recipes done with Latino flavors, or Mexican postres in an American mood. They represent the palate many Mexican Americans have developed by having roots in both countries. I call them my Chicana-proud desserts. Enjoy!

Introduction

Hi! I am Nicole Presley. I know—it's a curious name for a Mexican-American girl. I actually come from a long bloodline of Sandoval Guerreros (Mom's side) and Uribe Presleys (Dad's side)—"Presley" because my Nana Uribe married my Grandpa Presley.

Recently, my mom found the first book I wrote from preschool. Every page was dedicated to my desire to cook, bake, and be one with the kitchen. My vision was clear from a young age.

I started baking as a child out of a pure passion for food. I lived in a household among my adult Sandoval family, including my mom, my grandfather, and a few uncles and aunts. Everyone in my childhood home had amazing skills in the arts, but none in the culinary world. I didn't have anyone in my home guiding me in the kitchen, so I started teaching myself. Baking and cooking quickly became *my* art. Creating in the kitchen was my own private Shangri-la bubble, blocking out the world around me. Lucky for me, I was naturally good at baking. My taste buds were the critics I was most eager to please.

It wasn't long before I realized that the precision of measurements mixed together could be turned into a special treat that my family would love and appreciate. I come from a family of serious dessert lovers, so naturally they encouraged this baking love of mine.

I became obsessed with baking and learning any tidbits from the masters around me. My teachers were mostly older Mexican women who found my childhood fascination with the *cocina* (kitchen) charming and let me be involved, even if it was just to measure ingredients. Sometimes I would sit and watch and other times I was the novice helper, eager to run home afterward to try to recreate the dessert or dish until I felt it was ingrained in me. That's where my journey into the baking world began: completely self-taught.

By the time I was a young adult, I was confident in my dessert making and became known among creatives as a baker specializing in Mexican *postres* (desserts). I took my recipes/food art online and started a blog, opening a world I had never imagined for myself. My recipes and love of food soon caught the attention of some of the largest international brands. I was hired as a recipe developer by companies such as Disney,

Nestlé, Walmart, General Mills, and Idaho Potato, landing my work on their websites. These opportunities ushered in consulting jobs, food styling work on productions, spokesperson videos with countless companies, and recipe features in publications. I was even invited to the White House as a Latina food influencer! I am so grateful for every step my craft has taken me in this journey, and I look forward to what the future holds.

My work and passion for food are a huge part of who I am. Born and raised in East Los Angeles, California, I'm an American girl with deep roots in Mexico. I live comfortably between my dual cultures and celebrate them equally. This book is a love letter to my roots: my community of East LA, and the sweets I was raised on. You will find traditional Mexican desserts and some Latinized American *postres* too! By documenting these recipes, I hope to keep the Mexican traditions I grew up with alive for future generations and humbly pass down the knowledge I picked up from various kitchens both in Los Angeles and in Mexico. As food evolves, I hope people will be able to use this book as a resource to some truly FLANTASTIC desserts!

What You'll Find in My Pantry

Ate de Membrillo: See *membrillo.*

Baker's sugar: Instead of using granulated sugar, I like to use baker's sugar (also known as castor sugar) for its superfine texture. It melts easily and incorporates into doughs and batters easily. If you don't have baker's sugar, granulated will work fine, but this is definitely my preference.

Cajeta: A caramel sauce made from goat's milk. It can be found at any Mexican market. My favorite brand to use, and the one most commonly found in the United States, is Coronado. I use *cajeta* as the base of my flan. It is a time-saver and adds another element of creaminess to my flan. I also pipe it into my Peanut Butter *Cajeta* Cookies (page 57).

Cornstarch: Cornstarch is the secret thickening agent behind fruit fillings for empanadas and pie. It also plays a key role in making *atole* (page 156).

Dried hibiscus flowers: Also known as *flor de Jamaica.* Hibiscus flower is purchased dried, and when added to water it makes a sweet and tangy maroon-colored tea. I use hibiscus to flavor icings and dye them pink. I also use it as one of the many layers in my *ponche* (page 145).

Flavor extracts: Having a variety of extracts in the pantry really allows me to play with the flavor of baked goods, giving the final result a subtle taste of the extract used. I keep Mexican vanilla, orange, and almond extract in my pantry at all times, and I also use pistachio extract in this book.

Gel food coloring: I achieve the best color with gel food coloring. Having a small kit of your favorite colors allows for playful creations in the kitchen.

Marías cookies: These thin, dry everyday cookies come packaged in a box with rolls of around thirty cookies. They have a long storage life, are somewhat similar to a plain graham cracker, and sometimes go by the name of Marie Biscuits. They can be found at any Mexican and some American markets, and if not there, online. I use these cookies in my Cherry Carlota (page 77).

Mazapán: I think of mazapán as a dry, crumbly, sweet peanut powder that can easily be incorporated into many types of desserts or simply enjoyed on its own. It is not the same thing as marzipan, even though the spellings are similar. De la Rosa is the most popular brand in both the United States and Mexico. This delicious peanut candy is a staple in my house and made its way into my donut recipe (page 89).

Membrillo: *Membrillo* is known in English as quince. It's a type of fruit and can be found in the produce section of any Mexican market or online. I use *membrillo* in my *ponche* (page 145). *Ate de membrillo* is quince that has been candied and made into a thick paste or jelly. It is very solid and can be used as a topper to breads or eaten on its own. I use sliced ate de membrillo to top my *Rosca de Reyes* (page 150). Look for it in some Mexican markets or online.

Mexican chocolate drink tablets and Mexican chocolate powder: At its most basic, Mexican chocolate is a variety of chocolate. It has a distinct taste and comes in the form of drink tablets and powder. Mexican chocolate drink tablets are easily found in the international aisle of most supermarkets or online. These authentic tablets are commonly used to create frothy Mexican hot chocolate. They have an unmistakable taste and appearance and are not meant to be eaten on their own. They are ideal for melting and flavoring. To get powder, you can buy it in powder form already (Abuelita brand) or grate a drink tablet to a fine powder.

Mexican cinnamon: Mexican cinnamon is known as *canela*. Part of the Ceylon family of cinnamon, it's long in size, is made up of thin fragile layers, and has a sweeter flavor than other varieties of cinnamon. I use it in many desserts, including as a base to enhance the flavor of all my drinks.

Piloncillo: These cones of unrefined pure cane sugar are lifelong tenants of my pantry. Some people call piloncillo the Mexican brown sugar, but it tastes nothing like brown sugar. With hints of caramel and rum, piloncillo is the ultimate Mexican sweetener. It is hard to measure and comes in two sizes: the small cone, which is 20 grams (0.7 ounces), or the larger and more commonly used 3-inch-tall cone, which is usually 226.8 grams (8 ounces).

Star anise: Star anise is a spice made from a dried fruit that is indeed in the shape of a star. Aside from how beautiful anise is in all its star-shaped glory, it is a wonderful way to bring a slight licorice flavor to desserts and drinks.

Sweetened condensed milk: When I think of sweetened condensed milk, I immediately think of La Lechera. I grew up using the La Lechera brand, and its quality I know I can trust. Sweetened condensed milk is easy to find in most markets throughout the United States. This is the ingredient I used the most for this book besides flour. A single can of sweetened condensed milk can also be made into an irresistible dulce de leche (page 105).

Tamarind pods: Also known as *tamarindo*. The sticky, fleshy seeded pulp is encased in an extremely thin bark-like shell (pod) that can be broken with very little effort in your hands. Bend and it will snap. Carefully remove all the outer shell, and inside you will find a pod of seeds held together by a large twig vein that runs down the spine of the pod. Remove the vein by simply pulling it away from the pod. The fleshy portion is the part used to make *ponche* (page 145) or *agua de tamarindo*.

Tejocote: Also known as hawthorn. I mostly see this yellow-orangey-red small, round fruit during the holiday season. It is also sold jarred in a thick syrup or in the frozen section of Mexican markets. It could be bought online fresh from specialty produce vendors like Melissa's Produce.

Turbinado cane sugar: This crystalized sugar is made from the molasses of the sugar cane. It is spun in a turbine, which creates large golden granules. I use this sugar often, from empanadas to the crust for my flan. It's super easy to find; all major markets carry it.

Special Equipment

Blender: A blender is key to making the flan mixture smooth and creamy. I also use it to make the center for the *flotatina* (page 114).

Bundt cake pan: A 12-cup Bundt cake pan is a must-have for Mexican desserts. I use mine for flan and *gelatinas*. I recommend the metal variety for its heat distribution and chilling factor.

Candy thermometer: When an exact temperature is needed in a pot, my favorite tool is the candy thermometer. Candy thermometers come in a wide range of different styles and are made from different types of materials. I prefer the type that clips directly onto the pot for accurate temperature readings during the entire cooking or frying process. I use mine when making churros or donuts.

Cookie cutter: Round cookie cutters are a great tool to have on hand for donuts and *bisquets*.

Cookie scoop with quick release: This tool helps make all your cookies uniform, which is critical to baking times. Cookies with different amounts of dough will all bake differently. I use a 1 1/2-tablespoon scoop.

Food processor: I prefer to use my food processor when making dough for empanadas or pie. It cuts the fat into the flour much quicker than a pastry blender and is a time-saver.

Mixer: I have several mixers in my house, but I find that my stand mixer is my most prized of them all. I use it to whisk, mix, and knead. I use the dough hook attachment to make *conchas* and *Rosca de Reyes* (page 150).

Molinillo: A molinillo is a wooden three-ringed whisk that is used to grind down Mexican chocolate drink tablets when making hot chocolate or *atole*. It is used by rubbing the handle back and forth between the palm of both hands, which helps froth the chocolate.

Oven thermometer: I feel an oven thermometer is mandatory. I tested these recipes on two different ovens, and the baking times were as different as night and day. One factor that affects baking times is where the heat source is coming from. Some ovens generate heat from the back, some from the bottom. Because everyone's oven is different, I find that having an oven thermometer ensures you are baking at the right temperature.

Pastry brush: I use a silicone pastry brush for my egg wash on empanadas, pies, *Bisquets* (page 94), and *Rosca de Reyes* (page 150).

Piping bags and tips: Piping bags and tips are the tools I use to decorate cakes and cookies with icing, whipped cream, meringue, or *cajeta*. I also use them to pipe churros and fill the center of donuts with *crema*.

Rolling pin, adjustable: I prefer a rolling pin with the measurement rings attached on the side. They keep you from rolling your dough too thin. You will get the perfect dough thickness every time.

Rosette iron: A rosette iron is needed to make *Buñuelos de Viento* (page 149). They can be found at Mexican markets during the holiday season. They are also easily found on the internet under the name "rosette iron," "timbale iron," or "*buñuelera.*"

Silicone baking mats: I not only use my silicone baking mats when making a batch of cookies or empanadas, I also use them to freeze churro dough on. The nonstick mat is a baker's essential and is reusable for longtime use.

Springform pan: A springform pan is great for making cheesecake (page 83) or Cherry Carlota (page 77). The detachable sides make it easier to remove your masterpiece from the pan without breaking your cake.

Torch: I use my torch to harden sugar on the top of my *Arroz con Leche* Brûlée (page 128) and to brown the top of the meringue when making pie.

Tortilla press: Tortilla presses can be used to make tortillas, but I also use mine to press out my *concha* sugar topping. It makes perfectly round sugar toppers.

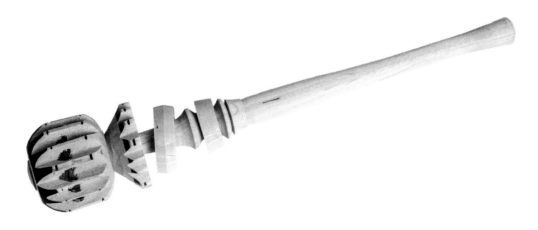

Flan Flan Flantastic

Coconut Almond Flan

If you love coconut, this is the flan for you. It's subtly sweet with a chewy layer of coconut that bakes into the flan and doubles down as a thin base. The slick accents of nuttiness come from the almonds that insisted they belong in the mix too.

Prep Time: 20 minutes   Bake Time: 1 hour   Cool Time: 30 minutes   Chill Time: 4 hours   Yield: 6 ramekins

1. Preheat oven to 350 degrees. Boil several cups water, enough to fill a large glass baking dish partway.
2. Pour sugar into a heavy-bottomed saucepan over medium-high heat. Do not stir. Swirl sugar in pan to break up any sugar clumps. After a few minutes the sugar will start to melt. Once the sugar is melting, reduce heat to medium-low and cook, swirling occasionally, until all sugar turns a light copper color. It will take 10 to 15 minutes for the sugar to become caramel.
3. Evenly pour caramel into 6 ramekins, quickly swirling each ramekin to coat the entire bottom with caramel. Set to the side and allow to cool.
4. In a blender add all remaining ingredients. Blend 2 minutes or until smooth.
5. Pour 1 cup flan mixture into each ramekin over cooled caramel. Cover each ramekin with a piece of aluminum foil.
6. Place all covered ramekins in a large baking dish. Fill baking dish with about 1 1/2 inches boiling hot water. Bake for 1 hour.
7. Remove large baking dish from oven. Then carefully remove each ramekin from water bath and place on a clean surface to cool for 30 minutes.
8. Remove aluminum foil. Run a butter knife along the edge of each ramekin to loosen the flan from the dish. Place a small plate on top of each ramekin, then flip to invert flan onto the plate. Gently lift up each ramekin and allow all caramel to drip out onto flan. Chill in the fridge for at least 4 hours.
9. Decorate with shredded coconut and almonds, if desired.

INGREDIENTS

1 cup sugar
4 tablespoons (2 ounces) cream cheese, room temperature
1/4 cup raw almonds, plus more for garnish
5 eggs
3/4 cup sweetened coconut flakes, plus more for garnish
1 teaspoon almond extract
1 (14-ounce) can sweetened condensed milk
1 (13.5-ounce) can coconut milk

Crusted Peach Flan

This is a summer flan. I make it only at the height of peach season, when fresh peaches are sweet and plentiful. Adding a crust to this peachy flan is completely optional, but that one extra step adds an element of crunch to the super creamy flan and plays to the hint of peach flavor. It's absolutely delicious, and if I could have a slice every day in the summer, I would.

FLAN

1. Preheat oven to 350 degrees. Boil several cups water, enough to fill a large glass baking dish halfway.
2. Spray a 12-cup Bundt pan with nonstick baking spray. Fill the bottom with *cajeta*.
3. In a blender add remaining flan ingredients. Blend for 1 minute or until completely combined. Pour flan mixture over *cajeta*.
4. Cover pan with aluminum foil and place inside a large baking dish. Fill baking dish halfway with boiling hot water. Place on bottom rack of oven and bake for 1 hour 10 minutes.
5. Remove from water bath and uncover. Run a small knife around the edge to prevent sticking, then let rest for 1 hour.

COOKIE CRUST

1. Place cookies in a food processor or a large ziplock bag. Pulse or crush until they become crumbs. You should have about 1 cup cookie crumbs.
2. If working with a food processor, add sugar and butter and pulse until fully incorporated.
3. If working with a ziplock bag, place cookie crumbs in a big bowl and mix in sugar. Massage butter into cookie crumbs with fingers until fully incorporated.
4. Cookie crust mixture should clump when squeezed together. Set to the side until ready to use.

ASSEMBLY

1. Firmly press cookie crumbs on top of the flan in the pan to create crust. Allow flan to rest for an additional 2 hours at room temperature.
2. Flip flan over onto a plate. Slowly lift pan up away from plate. Chill in the fridge for 6 hours or overnight.

INGREDIENTS

Flan
1/2 cup *cajeta*
2 large peaches, pitted
1 (14-ounce) can sweetened condensed milk
1 (12-ounce) can evaporated milk
5 eggs
5 tablespoons (2.5 ounces) cream cheese, room temperature
1/4 cup brown sugar
1/2 tablespoon Mexican vanilla extract

Cookie Crust
10 to 12 graham crackers or almond cookies
3 tablespoons turbinado sugar
3 tablespoons butter

Chocolate Banana Flan

I call this chocolate banana flan *El Changuito* (The Little Monkey)! This flan is no monkey business even though it will have you swinging from tree to tree and begging for more.

Prep Time: 10 minutes   Bake Time: 1 hour 10 minutes   Rest Time: 2 hours   Chill Time: 6 hours or overnight   Yield: 12 servings

1. Preheat oven to 350 degrees. Boil several cups water, enough to fill a large glass baking dish halfway.
2. Spray a 12-cup Bundt pan with nonstick baking spray. Pour *cajeta* into pan.
3. In a blender add all remaining ingredients except chocolate chips. Blend for 1 minute or until completely combined.
4. Pour flan mixture over *cajeta*, then sprinkle chocolate chips evenly over the top. Chocolate chips will sink to the bottom of the pan.
5. Cover pan with aluminum foil and place inside a large baking dish. Fill baking dish halfway with boiling hot water. Place on bottom rack of oven and bake for 1 hour 10 minutes.
6. Remove flan from water bath and uncover. Let rest for 2 hours.
7. Run a small knife around the edge. Flip flan over onto a plate. Slowly lift pan up. Chill in the fridge 6 hours or overnight.

INGREDIENTS

1/2 cup *cajeta*
5 eggs
5 tablespoons (2.5 ounces) cream cheese, room temperature
2 large ripe bananas
1 (14-ounce) can sweetened condensed milk
1 (12-ounce) can evaporated milk
1/2 tablespoon Mexican vanilla extract
1/8 teaspoon salt
1 cup chocolate chips

Mini Choco-Flan

Choco-flan is also know as impossible cake. It must be assembled in order for the flan to end up on top when the cake is inverted onto a plate: first cajeta, second cake batter, and third flan mixture. The flan will magically sink to the bottom of the pan during the baking process. Magical and delicious!

Prep Time: 30 minutes   Bake Time: 45 minutes per pan (3 pans)   Rest Time: 2 hours   Chill Time: 6 hours or overnight   Yield: 30 mini choco-flans

1. Preheat oven to 350 degrees. Boil several cups water, enough to fill a large glass baking dish halfway.
2. Spray 3 cupcake pans (30 compartments; see tip) with nonstick baking spray. Pour 1 teaspoon *cajeta* or caramel into the bottom of each cupcake compartment.

CAKE

1. To prepare cinnamon tea, in a saucepan bring water and cinnamon sticks to a boil, then remove from heat and steep for 10 minutes.
2. In a mixing bowl, combine flour, cocoa powder, baking soda, baking powder, and sugar. Add vegetable oil, eggs, vanilla, and buttermilk. Mix on medium for 2 minutes, then on medium-high for 2 more minutes. Pour in 3/4 cup hot tea and mix until fully combined.
3. Fill each cupcake compartment with 2 tablespoons cake batter.

FLAN

1. In a blender add all flan ingredients. Blend on medium for 2 minutes.
2. Fill each cupcake compartment with 2 1/2 tablespoons flan.

BAKING

1. Spray three large pieces of aluminum foil (enough to cover the top of each cupcake pan) with nonstick baking spray. Loosely place sprayed aluminum foil on top of the cupcake pans.
2. Place one covered cupcake pan in a large baking dish. Fill baking dish halfway with boiling hot water. Place in oven on middle rack and bake for 45 minutes or until toothpick comes out clean. Repeat with remaining two pans.
3. Remove cupcake pan from baking dish and remove aluminum foil. Let cool in the pan for 2 hours.
4. Run a butter knife along the edge of each cupcake compartment. Flip pan over onto a plate. Slowly lift pan up away from plate. Chill in the fridge for 6 hours or overnight. Serve chilled.

Tip: When filling the cupcake pans, fill the outer cup cavities only, leaving the two in the center empty. The two center cups do not bake as evenly as the outside cups.

INGREDIENTS

1/2 cup plus 2 tablespoons (30 teaspoons) *cajeta* or caramel

Cake
1 1/2 cups water
2 Mexican cinnamon sticks
2 cups flour
1/2 cup cocoa powder, packed
1 teaspoon baking soda
1 teaspoon baking powder
2 cups sugar
1/2 cup vegetable oil
2 eggs
1 teaspoon Mexican vanilla extract
1 cup buttermilk

Flan
5 eggs
1 (14-ounce) can sweetened condensed milk
1 (12-ounce) can evaporated milk
1 teaspoon Mexican vanilla extract
5 tablespoons (2.5 ounces) cream cheese, room temperature

Strawberry Pistachio Flan

Strawberry pistachio flan is the kind of dessert you would serve to a queen in spring! This flan is capable of making anyone feel special. It tastes like a cross between cheesecake, mousse, and flan.

I could eat this flan all day. Making the batch into individual cups sure helps me share the flan easily or eat a little at a time. You could also skip on making it into individual cups and pour the mixture into a 12-cup Bundt pan instead, with the same cooking time.

Prep Time: 20 minutes   Bake Time: 1 hour   Rest Time: 2 hours   Chill Time: 6 hours or overnight   Yield: 8 servings

1. Preheat oven to 350 degrees. Boil several cups water, enough to fill a large glass baking dish halfway.
2. Spray 8 (6-ounce) glass custard cups with nonstick baking spray. Fill the bottom of each cup with 1 tablespoon *cajeta*.
3. In a blender add all remaining ingredients except 1/4 cup pistachios. Blend for 1 minute or until completely combined.
4. Pour evenly among baking cups. Sprinkle the tops with remaining 1/4 cup pistachios.
5. Cover cups with aluminum foil and place inside a large baking dish. Fill baking dish halfway with boiling hot water. Bake for 1 hour.
6. Remove cups from water bath and uncover. Let rest for 2 hours.
7. Invert cups onto a plate. Slowly lift cups up away from plate. Chill in the fridge for 6 hours or overnight.

INGREDIENTS

1/2 cup *cajeta*
1/4 cup sugar
5 large eggs
3/4 cup (6 ounces) cream cheese, room temperature
1/2 tablespoon pistachio extract
1/2 tablespoon Mexican vanilla extract
1 (14-ounce) can sweetened condensed milk
1 (12-ounce) can evaporated milk
1 cup strawberries, stems removed
3/4 cup shelled and roughly chopped pistachios, divided

Empanadas y Pay
(Empanadas and Pie)

Empanada and Pie Dough

This recipe yields two disks of dough. One disk is needed for a single pie crust; use the second if the pie has a crust on the top. One disk makes six empanadas; both disks together make twelve.

Prep Time: 20 minutes   Chill Time: overnight   Yield: 2 dough disks

1. Place flour, sugar, and salt into a food processor. Pulse to combine.
2. Add vegetable shortening and cream cheese. Pulse until both fats are cut into flour.
3. Add butter in three parts, pulsing after each addition. Do not overpulse. You are looking for pea-sized balls of butter to remain.
4. Add cold water 1 tablespoon at a time. Pulse once between each addition.
5. Dump dough onto a clean surface. Run hands under cold water for a few minutes. Dry hands well, then quickly press dough together to form a long log. Divide the log in half, and form each half into a disk. Wrap each disk in plastic wrap and place in the fridge overnight.

Tip: To make vegan dough, use plant-based unsalted butter and replace cream cheese with an extra 1/4 cup butter (1 1/4 cups butter total).

Tip: If you do not have a food processor, grate frozen cream cheese and butter before adding them to the flour. This will save time from using a pastry cutter.

INGREDIENTS

3 cups all-purpose flour
1/4 cup sugar
1 1/2 teaspoons salt
1/3 cup vegetable shortening, spooned into teaspoon drops and frozen
2 ounces cream cheese, frozen
1 cup butter, cut into tabs and frozen
1/2 cup ice-cold water

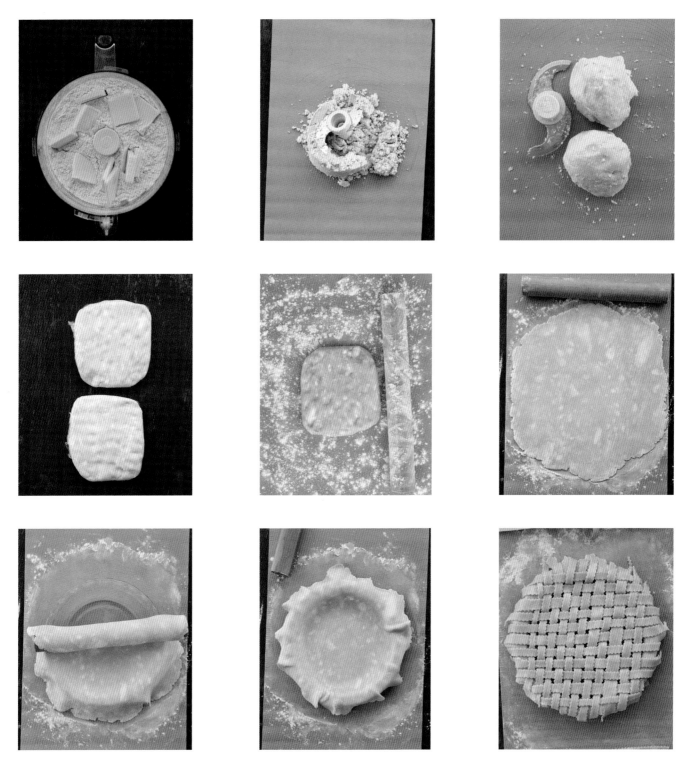

Marranito Pear Empanadas

Marranitos are Mexican gingerbread cookies shaped like pigs. In my house, we call this type of *pan dulce* "Piggy Pan." I decided to pay homage to the molasses pig with a marranito pear-stuffed empanada! I make these the second I feel a little chill in the air and pears are in season.

Prep Time: 1 hour   Chill Time: overnight   Bake Time: 25 minutes   Yield: 13 empanadas

GINGERBREAD DOUGH

1. Add flour, ground cinnamon, baking powder, ground ginger, and brown sugar to a food processor. Pulse to mix completely. Add butter, vegetable shortening, eggs, and molasses. Pulse to bring dough completely together.
2. Remove dough from food processor and knead with hands to fully incorporate. Dough should not be sticky at all. Divide into 4 parts and flatten into disks. Wrap each disk in plastic wrap and refrigerate overnight.

PEAR FILLING

1. In a small bowl mix cold water and cornstarch until cornstarch dissolves. Set to the side.
2. In a heavy-bottomed pot over medium-high heat, add pear pieces, brown sugar, butter, salt, and vanilla. Bring to a boil, stirring occasionally, about 15 minutes.
3. Add whipping cream and mix to fully incorporate cream with sugar. Cook for 10 minutes.
4. Pour cornstarch mixture into pear mixture and mix until thickened. Remove from heat and allow to cool to room temperature.

ASSEMBLY

1. Preheat oven to 350 degrees. Prepare egg wash by mixing egg and water together. Set to the side.
2. On a generously floured surface, roll out gingerbread dough to a 1/16-inch thickness. With a piggy cookie cutter, cut out as many cookie shapes as possible, rerolling scraps and cutting until all dough is used. You will need 2 cutouts for each empanada (26 total cookies for 13 empanadas).

INGREDIENTS

Gingerbread Dough
3 cups flour
3 teaspoons ground cinnamon
1 teaspoon baking powder
3 teaspoons ground ginger
5 tablespoons dark brown sugar
3/4 cup salted butter
2 tablespoons vegetable shortening
2 large eggs
4 tablespoons dark molasses

Pear Filling
2 tablespoons cold water
1 1/2 tablespoons cornstarch
4 cups peeled, cored, and cubed
    pear (about 5 1/2 pears)
1 cup brown sugar
2 tablespoons butter
1/8 teaspoon salt
1/2 teaspoon Mexican vanilla extract
3 tablespoons heavy whipping cream

Egg Wash
1 egg
1 tablespoon water

Royal Icing
3 tablespoons meringue powder
4 cups confectioners' sugar
5 tablespoons milk
1 tablespoon warm water

3. Place half the gingerbread cutouts (13 cutouts) on a baking sheet lined with a nonstick baking mat. Place 1 tablespoon pear filling in the center of each gingerbread cutout and spread it just in the middle. With your finger, brush the outside rim of each gingerbread cutout with egg wash. Then top with another gingerbread cutout. With a fork, press down all along the edges to enclose the empanadas. Then brush the entire top of each empanada with egg wash.
4. Bake for 25 minutes.

ROYAL ICING

1. Mix all icing ingredients together until smooth.
2. Place in a piping bag with any tip.
3. Allow cookies to cool completely, then decorate with royal icing.

Piña Pie

When I was growing up, pineapple pie was the most common hand pie in my house. My grandfather lived for a good *empanada de piña*. He would come home after a hard day at work with a *bolsa* (bag) of a few empanadas from the *panadería* (bakery), and rest assured pineapple was always a part of the bag. I decided to pay tribute to his favorite pineapple filling and make a *pay de piña* for my beloved *abuelito* Sandoval.

Prep Time: 1 hour, not including dough prep   Bake Time: 1 hour 15 minutes   Chill Time: 5 hours or overnight   Yield: 1 (9 1/2-inch) pie

PINEAPPLE FILLING

1. Place sugars, pineapple chunks, cinnamon sticks, and 3/4 cup water in a stockpot over medium-high heat. Mix to combine completely. Bring to a boil and cook for 20 minutes.
2. After boiling, smash the pineapple a bit with the back of a spoon or potato masher to break it up into smaller pieces. Remove cinnamon sticks.
3. In a small bowl whisk remaining 1/4 cup water and cornstarch together until cornstarch dissolves. Slowly pour cornstarch mixture into pineapple mixture, mixing quickly until incorporated. Cook for 3 minutes, allowing mixture to thicken and glaze to become clear.
4. Remove from heat and let cool to room temperature.

ASSEMBLY

1. Preheat oven to 425 degrees with rack in the bottom third. Prepare egg wash by mixing egg and water together. Set to the side.
2. On a floured work space, roll out 1 dough disk a few inches larger than a 9 1/2-inch pie plate, to a 1/8-inch thickness. Carefully transfer dough to pie plate. Let edge hang over sides.
3. Fill with cooled filling.
4. Roll out second dough disk to a 1/8-inch thickness. Place over pineapple filling, designing however you'd like, as long as you make some sort of ventilation for the pie. I cut the dough into 1/4-inch-wide strips and then weaved it into a lattice top.

INGREDIENTS

Crust
2 disks pie dough (page 30)

Pineapple Filling
1 cup dark brown sugar or piloncillo
1/2 cup granulated sugar
6 cups cubed fresh pineapple
2 Mexican cinnamon sticks
1 cup water, divided
4 1/2 tablespoons cornstarch

Egg Wash
1 egg
1 tablespoon water

Crust Topping
1/4 cup turbinado sugar

5. Fold top crust over bottom crust at the edge of the pie rim and pinch together. Make a pattern with your fingers or decorate with a fork pattern.

6. Using a pastry brush, lightly brush top of pie and edges with egg wash. Sprinkle top with turbinado sugar.

7. Place pie plate on a cookie sheet. Bake for 25 minutes.

8. Remove pie from oven and place an aluminum foil tent around the edge of the crust only. This will keep the edge from burning but allow the center to continue to brown.

9. Reduce oven heat to 375 degrees. Bake for 50 minutes.

10. Allow to cool for a minimum of 4 to 5 hours, but overnight is ideal. Enjoy!

Tip: I like to roll my dough on a nonstick baking sheet. Roll the dough out from the center and rotate the mat as you roll to make a perfect circle.

Tip: There are a few methods of placing the dough into the pie plate. You can roll the dough around your rolling pin, then unroll it onto the plate. Or you can fold it into fourths and unfold it onto the plate. Either method works. I like the rolling pin method.

Candied Pumpkin Empanadas

Candied pumpkin empanadas make a lovely addition to the Thanksgiving table. Even though they are a handheld dessert, you can be fancy and serve them on a plate with a fork and knife. Pair them with a warm cozy cup of Cinnamon *Atole* (page 156), which gets along with these pumpkin spice hand pies like a house on fire. The fall season will never be the same.

Prep Time: 30 minutes, not including pumpkin and dough prep   Bake Time: 20 minutes   Yield: 12 empanadas

1. Once pumpkin slices come to room temperature, remove pumpkin slices from piloncillo syrup. With your fingers carefully remove peel from pumpkin flesh. Discard peel and place flesh in a bowl. Mash with a fork to create a smooth purée. Set to the side.
2. Preheat oven to 425 degrees. Line a baking sheet with parchment paper or a nonstick baking mat. Set to the side.
3. On a floured surface, roll each dough disk to a 1/8-inch thickness (14x12-inch rectangle). Cut each rectangle into 6 equal parts (12 parts total).
4. Fill each piece of dough with 2 tablespoons pumpkin filling. Carefully pull one corner of the dough to the opposite corner to enclose pumpkin filling and create a triangle shape. With your finger press the ends of the dough together. Then roll the ends of the dough an inch toward the pumpkin center to really enforce the closure, but keep the triangle shape. (See following page for images of the process.)
5. Place empanadas 2 inches apart on prepared baking sheet. Prepare egg wash by mixing egg and water. Brush each empanada with egg wash and sprinkle with turbinado sugar and ground cinnamon. Make 3 little slits on each empanada with a small paring knife to allow ventilation.
6. Bake for 20 minutes or until golden brown on top. Place on cooling rack and allow to come to room temperature. Serve with *atole*.

INGREDIENTS

cooked pumpkin slices from *Calabaza en Tacha* (page 142)
2 disks empanada dough (page 30)

Egg Wash
1 egg
1 tablespoon water

Toppings
turbinado sugar for sprinkling
ground cinnamon for sprinkling

Cherry *Jamaica* (Hibiscus) Empanadas

These cherry *Jamaica* empanadas give new meaning to a Mexican-American fusion dessert. A flaky crust envelops a decadent cherry filling, and once the empanadas are baked, they are baptized with a drizzle of sweet hibiscus glaze. Yes, please.

Prep Time: 1 hour, not including dough prep   Cool Time: 5 hours plus 1 hour   Bake Time: 22 minutes   Yield: 12 empanadas

FILLING

1. Wash and pit cherries.
2. Place cherries, sugar, almond extract, lemon juice, and salt in a heavy-bottomed saucepan over medium-low heat. Mix to combine all ingredients and cook for about 25 minutes.
3. After boiling, smash cherries with the back of a mixing spoon to break them up a bit.
4. Mix cornstarch and water together until easy to stir and cornstarch is dissolved. Pour cornstarch mixture over boiling cherries and mix until completely combined. Mixture will start to thicken. Continue mixing for an additional 3 minutes or until you have a thick glaze.
5. Remove from heat and allow to cool for a minimum of 5 hours.

ASSEMBLY

1. Whisk egg and water together in a small bowl to create an egg wash. Set to the side.
2. Preheat oven to 425 degrees. Line a baking sheet with parchment paper or a nonstick baking mat. Set to the side.
3. On a floured surface, roll each dough disk to a 1/8-inch thickness (14x12-inch rectangle). Cut each rectangle into 6 equal parts (12 parts total).
4. Fill each piece of dough with 2 tablespoons cherry filling. Then carefully pull one end of the dough to the other end of dough to enclose cherry filling and create a triangle

INGREDIENTS

2 disks empanada dough (page 30)

Filling
2 pounds cherries (about 6 cups)
3/4 cup sugar
1 teaspoon almond extract
1/2 teaspoon lemon juice
pinch of salt
2 tablespoons cornstarch
2 tablespoons cold water

Egg Wash
1 egg
1 tablespoon water

Hibiscus Glaze
1/4 cup dried hibiscus flowers
1/2 cup boiling hot water
2 cups confectioners' sugar

shape. With your finger press the ends of the dough together. Then roll the ends of the dough an inch toward the cherry center to really enforce the closure, but keep the triangle shape.

5. Place empanadas 2 inches apart on prepared baking sheet. Take a floured fork and crimp the edges of the dough. Brush each empanada with egg wash. Make 3 little slits on each empanada with a small paring knife to allow ventilation.

6. Bake for 20 to 22 minutes or until golden brown on top. Place on cooling rack and allow to come to room temperature.

HIBISCUS GLAZE

1. Steep hibiscus flowers in hot water for 15 minutes. Strain through a sieve and discard hibiscus leaves.

2. Place confectioners' sugar in a bowl. Whisk in 6 tablespoons of hibiscus water.

3. Drizzle or spoon hibiscus glaze over each empanada. Allow glaze to set and harden for 1 hour. Enjoy!

Tip: I like to vary how I spoon or drizzle the hibiscus glaze over each empanada to give every one a unique look.

Tip: Veganize this recipe by making vegan empanada dough (see tip on page 30), and instead of egg wash, brush with almond milk or coconut milk.

Dulce de Leche Pumpkin Pie

Can we really welcome the holiday season into our homes without the addition of pumpkin pie? This dulce de leche pumpkin pie covered in a meringue sauce combines traditional pumpkin pie and dulce de leche together in match-made-in-the-kitchen matrimony.

Prep Time: 45 minutes, not including dough prep   *Bake Time: 1 hour 5 minutes*   *Yield: 1 (9 1/2-inch) pie*

CRUST

1. Preheat oven to 425 degrees. Prepare egg wash by mixing together egg and water. Set to the side.
2. On a floured work space, roll out 1 dough disk larger than a 9 1/2-inch pie plate, to a 1/4-inch thickness. Carefully transfer dough to pie plate. Let edge hang over sides, then tuck edge under itself and crimp with your fingers. Brush edge with egg wash.
3. Fit a large piece of parchment paper in the center of the pie. Fill with 2 pounds dried beans or pie weights to keep the pie crust from puffing up. Bake for 15 minutes. Remove beans and parchment paper and bake for an additional 5 minutes. Remove from oven and allow blind-baked crust to cool.
4. Either save remaining dough disk for another pie or use to decorate top of pie. Roll out to a 1/4-inch thickness and cut out shapes with cookie cutters. Bake cutout pieces of dough on a baking sheet for 15 to 20 minutes at 425 degrees. Set to the side.

DULCE DE LECHE PUMPKIN FILLING

1. In a blender combine all filling ingredients. Blend until completely puréed.
2. Place pie plate with blind-baked pie crust on a cookie sheet to make it easier to place in the oven. Cover the edges of the crust with aluminum foil to ensure they do not overbrown while baking.
3. Pour pumpkin filling into crust and bake at 425 degrees for 15 minutes. Lower temperature to 350 degrees and bake for an additional 35 minutes.

INGREDIENTS

Crust
1 or 2 disks pie dough (page 30; see crust directions)

Egg Wash
1 egg
1 tablespoon water

Dulce de Leche Pumpkin Filling
1 (14-ounce) can sweetened condensed milk
1 cup evaporated milk
1 1/2 teaspoons pumpkin pie spice
1/2 teaspoon salt
3 eggs
1 (15-ounce) can pumpkin purée
1 teaspoon Mexican vanilla extract

Meringue Sauce
4 egg whites
1 1/3 cups baker's sugar

4. Turn off oven and leave oven door ajar. Let pie rest in oven for 30 minutes to cool slightly. Remove from oven and allow to cool to room temperature.

MERINGUE SAUCE

1. Mix egg whites and sugar in a double boiler on low heat. Mix constantly with a whisk until you can no longer see the sugar granules or until the temperature on a candy thermometer reaches 150 degrees.
2. Transfer meringue to a stand mixer fitted with the whisk attachment. Mix on high until it barely peaks and then quickly loses its shape, about 2 minutes.
3. Place in a piping bag fitted with a star tip. Design meringue on top of pie.
4. Optional: With a torch on a low or medium flame, toast the top of the meringue for a golden look.
5. Decorate with pie crust cutouts, if desired.
6. Meringue will spill down the sides of the pie when cut and will act like a sauce. Enjoy!

Apple Empanadas

This beautiful dessert takes the apple empanada to the next level of sophistication! The piloncillo almond filling flavors the apple on the inside, and dulce de leche ties all the flavors together on the outside.

Prep Time: 20 minutes, not including dough prep   Chill Time: 20 minutes   Bake Time: 1 hour 45 minutes   Yield: 6 empanadas

PILONCILLO ALMOND BUTTER

1. In a small mixing bowl, combine all piloncillo almond butter ingredients. Mix until fully incorporated. Set to the side.

APPLES

1. Preheat oven to 350 degrees.
2. Core apples by cutting out a 1-inch circle at the bottom of each apple with a paring knife or a metal 1/4 teaspoon implement. Scrape out the center of each apple until all seeds are removed, leaving the stem intact.
3. Peel apples with a vegetable peeler, removing all skin.
4. Using a butter knife or small spoon, fill each apple cavity with piloncillo almond butter.
5. Place filled apples in a baking dish. Add water to baking dish and bake for 1 hour 20 minutes or until apples are fork-tender. Remove from oven and allow to cool to room temperature overnight.

INGREDIENTS

2 disks pie dough (page 30)
dulce de leche (page 105)

Piloncillo Almond Butter
4 tablespoons butter, room temperature
1/4 cup ground piloncillo, packed
1/8 teaspoon ground cinnamon
1/2 teaspoon orange extract
1/4 cup sliced almonds

Apples
6 firm apples
4 tablespoons water

Egg Wash
1 egg
1 tablespoon water

ASSEMBLY

1. Line a baking sheet with a nonstick baking mat. Set to the side.
2. To prepare egg wash, whisk egg and water together in a small bowl. Set to the side.
3. Roll 1 disk pie dough to a 14x12-inch rectangle. Cut into 3 triangles. The easiest way to cut into 3 triangles is to find the middle point of the long side and use that as the top of the center triangle. Cut two diagonal lines from that middle point to the opposite corners. You will be left with a triangle on either side of the center triangle. Repeat with remaining dough disk.
4. Place 1 cooled apple into the center of a triangle. Using a pastry brush, brush the edges of the dough with egg wash. Then carefully bring each point of the dough to the top of the apple. Leaving the stem exposed, pinch the seams together to cover the apple completely. Repeat with remaining apples and dough.

5. Place covered apples 2 inches apart on prepared baking sheet. Brush with egg wash. Place in refrigerator to chill for 20 minutes.
6. Heat oven to 425 degrees. Bake for 20 to 25 minutes or until golden brown.
7. Remove from oven and allow to cool for 10 minutes. Drizzle each apple with dulce de leche and enjoy!

Tip: To ground piloncillo, I break a piloncillo cone into smaller pieces with a mallet and then grind the pieces in a food processor or blender.

Tip: If you're wondering which type of apple to use, I used Granny Smith and Pink Lady.

Galletas
(Cookies)

Peanut Butter *Cajeta* Cookies

This balanced amount of sweet, salty, and crisp comes straight out of the cookie playbook and directly to your favorite peanut butter cookie list. You can freeze half the dough rolled into balls for a later date or for impromptu cookie cravings.

Prep Time: 30 minutes   *Chill Time: 1 hour*   *Bake Time: 15 minutes per baking sheet*   *Yield: 4 1/2 dozen cookies*

1. Preheat oven to 350 degrees. Line a baking sheet with a nonstick baking mat. Set to the side.
2. In a stand mixer fitted with the paddle attachment, cream sugars and butter for about 4 minutes or until fluffy. Add almond extract and eggs and mix until combined. Add peanut butter and mix until well combined.
3. In a separate bowl sift flour, baking soda, baking powder, and salt together. Add flour mixture to peanut butter mixture. Mix just to combine.
4. Add chopped peanuts and mix to combine.
5. Refrigerate dough for 1 hour; this will help the cookies hold their shape.
6. Scoop dough into uniform balls by using a 1 1/2-tablespoon cookie scoop and rolling each ball in your hands to make the shape more round. (Note: If freezing dough, do so now.)
7. Drop balls into a small bowl of sugar and coat completely. Place on prepared baking sheet 2 inches apart. Firmly press fork tines into opposite sides of each ball of dough to make ridges (like a skeleton ribcage).
8. Bake for 14 minutes for a slightly soft center or 15 minutes for a crispier cookie. Remove from baking sheet and place on a cooling rack.
9. Place *cajeta* in a piping bag fitted with a very small tip. Once cookies have cooled, pipe little drops of *cajeta* into the ridges and enjoy!

   Tip: To freeze dough, place scooped balls of dough onto a baking mat and freeze. Once frozen, place balls of dough in a freezer-safe ziplock bag. To bake frozen dough, defrost and bring to room temperature, then follow steps from coating in sugar to the end.

INGREDIENTS

1 cup brown sugar
3/4 cup sugar, plus more for dusting
1 cup salted butter, room temperature
1 teaspoon almond extract
2 eggs
1 cup creamy peanut butter
2 1/2 cups flour
1 teaspoon baking soda
1/2 teaspoon baking powder
1/4 teaspoon salt
3/4 cup salted peanuts, coarsely chopped
1/2 cup *cajeta*

Mexican Chocolate Cookies

These cookies are made up of all the key elements of Mexican hot chocolate. Chocolate and cinnamon give these *galletas* the taste most Latino children grow up on, and the addition of pine nuts complements the familiar flavors immaculately. These are great cookies to keep in the cookie jar or to bake as gifts for beloved chocolate lovers.

Prep Time: 20 minutes   Chill Time: 3 hours   Bake Time: 15 minutes per baking sheet   Yield: 2 1/2 dozen cookies

1. In a mixer on medium speed, cream butter and sugars together for 3 minutes or until mixture looks light and fluffy. Add egg and vanilla. Mix until fully combined.
2. In a separate bowl whisk together flour, cocoa powder, ground cinnamon, and baking soda. Add dry ingredients to wet ingredients and mix on medium until dough comes together.
3. Mix in pine nuts until just combined.
4. Place cookie dough in refrigerator for 3 hours to chill.
5. Preheat oven to 350 degrees. Line a baking sheet with a nonstick baking mat. Set to the side.
6. Scoop dough into uniform balls by using a 1 1/2-tablespoon cookie scoop and rolling each ball in your hands to make the shape more round.
7. Dip each ball of cookie dough in grated Mexican chocolate and place 2 inches apart on prepared baking sheet. Bake for 15 minutes.
8. Allow to cool on baking sheet for 5 minutes before removing to a cooling rack. Allow cookies to come to room temperature.
9. To make ganache, add whipping cream to a small saucepan and cook over medium-low heat. Once little bubbles form around the edge of the pan, add Mexican chocolate powder. Stir with a rubber spatula until mixture becomes smooth and is completely combined.
10. Dip half of each cookie into ganache. Let excess drip off, then place on a cooling rack to harden overnight.

INGREDIENTS

1 cup butter, room temperature
3/4 cup dark brown sugar
3/4 cup sugar
1 egg
1 teaspoon Mexican vanilla extract
1 1/2 cups flour
1/2 cup unsweetened cocoa powder
1 teaspoon ground cinnamon
1 teaspoon baking soda
1/2 cup pine nuts
1 disk Mexican chocolate, grated

Mexican Chocolate Ganache
1 cup heavy whipping cream
2 cups Mexican chocolate powder

Abue Herminia's Oatmeal Cookies

My great-grandmother Herminia lived on both sides of the El Paso–Juárez border at different times in her life, and she used to make these fabulous crispy, chewy oatmeal cookies. By the time I was born, she was no longer sharing her craft in the kitchen, but my grandfather used to make these cookies with the guidance of his mother. He said they tasted just like home, and they do.

Prep Time: 30 minutes   Bake Time: 15 minutes per baking sheet   Yield: 4 dozen cookies

1. Preheat oven to 325 degrees. Line a baking sheet with parchment paper. Set to the side.
2. In a stand mixer on medium-high speed, cream sugars and butter for 3 minutes or until fluffy, stopping midway to scrape down butter.
3. Add vanilla and almond extracts and mix to incorporate. Add eggs one at a time until fully incorporated.
4. In a separate bowl, mix flour, wheat germ, baking soda, baking powder, ground cinnamon, salt, and oats. Add dry ingredients to wet ingredients. Mix on medium-low to combine.
5. Fold in raisins and pecans.
6. Scoop 2 tablespoons cookie dough into a ball and place on prepared baking sheet. Flatten slightly with the back of a spoon. Repeat so there are 6 cookies per baking sheet.
7. Bake for 15 minutes. Allow to cool on baking sheet for 5 minutes before removing to a cooling rack.

Tip: I cook two trays at a time so the baking time doesn't take so long.

INGREDIENTS

1 1/3 cups dark brown sugar
1 1/3 cups baker's sugar
1 1/2 cups salted butter
1 teaspoon Mexican vanilla extract
1/2 teaspoon almond extract
3 eggs
2 cups plus 2 tablespoons flour
1/2 cup wheat germ
1 1/2 teaspoons baking soda
2 teaspoons baking powder
3/4 teaspoon ground cinnamon
1/2 teaspoon salt
3 1/4 cups old-fashioned oats
1 cup golden raisins
3/4 cup chopped pecans

Sprinkle Cookies

Step to the side, Mexican cookie staple coming through . . . Sprinkle cookies are an everyday cookie there to comfort you any time of the year. These buttery candied *galletas con grageas* (sprinkle cookies) are easy to make and remind me of all the *panaderías* (bakeries) I have visited in East Los Angeles and deep in the heart of Mexico.

Prep Time: 15 minutes   Chill Time: 30 minutes   Bake Time: 15 minutes per baking sheet   Yield: 2 1/2 dozen cookies

1. Line a baking sheet with a nonstick baking mat. Set to the side.
2. Sift flour, salt, baking powder, and baking soda together in a bowl. Set to the side.
3. In a stand mixer fitted with the paddle attachment, cream butter and sugar on medium speed until creamy. Add whole egg, egg yolk, and vanilla. Beat until fully combined.
4. Reduce speed to low and gradually mix in flour mixture until fully combined.
5. Scoop dough into uniform balls by using a 1 1/2-tablespoon cookie scoop and rolling each ball in your hands to make the shape more round.
6. Whisk all egg wash ingredients together in a small bowl. Lightly brush cookie tops with glossy egg wash, then dip in sprinkles to adhere. Place on prepared baking sheet 2 inches apart. With the top of a plate or glass, flatten each cookie down to a 1/4-inch thickness.
7. Refrigerate tray of cookies for 30 minutes.
8. Heat oven to 350 degrees. Bake for 15 minutes or until sides and middle are set.
9. Remove from oven and place cookie sheet on wire rack. Allow cookies to cool completely.

INGREDIENTS

2 1/2 cups flour
1/8 teaspoon salt
1 teaspoon baking powder
1 teaspoon baking soda
1 cup butter, room temperature
1 cup plus 2 tablespoons sugar
1 whole egg plus 1 egg yolk
1 teaspoon Mexican vanilla extract
4 ounces nonpareils sprinkles

Glossy Egg Wash
1 egg
1/16 teaspoon salt
1/16 teaspoon sugar

Pasteles
(Cakes)

Coconut *Piña* Celebration Cake

It's not a real party until the coconut pineapple cake is cut. This delicious layer cake is moist, sweet, and creamy—or should I say dreamy. Layers of fresh pineapple filling are sandwiched between layers of coconut cake and topped with a simple buttercream icing. I make this cake for special occasions and on days when I need to deliver a big smile to someone's face.

Prep Time: 45 minutes | *Bake Time: 35 minutes* | *Cool Time: 4 hours plus 30 minutes* | *Assembly Time: 20 minutes* | *Yield: 12 servings*

CAKE

1. Preheat oven to 325 degrees. Spray 3 (9-inch) round cake pans with nonstick baking spray, then line the bottoms with parchment paper. Set to the side.
2. Beat vegetable oil, sugar, eggs, vanilla, and almond extract in a stand mixer on medium speed until well combined. It will look like a thick pale-yellow gel.
3. In a separate bowl sift flour, baking soda, salt, and ground cinnamon together. Slowly add flour mixture to egg mixture and mix until fully incorporated.
4. Reduce speed to low and add buttermilk. Mix until well combined. Add coconut and mix until evenly distributed.
5. Pour 2 1/4 cups batter into each prepared pan. Bake for 35 minutes or until toothpick comes out clean. Allow to cool in pan until cakes come to room temperature.

PINEAPPLE FILLING

1. Place piloncillo, sugar, pineapple chunks, cinnamon sticks, salt, and 1/2 cup water in a stockpot over medium-high heat and mix to combine completely. Bring to a boil and cook for 20 minutes.
2. After boiling, smash pineapple a bit with the back of a spoon or a potato masher to break it up into smaller pieces. Remove cinnamon sticks.
3. In a small bowl whisk remaining 1/4 cup cold water and cornstarch until cornstarch dissolves. Slowly pour cornstarch mixture into pineapple mixture, mixing

INGREDIENTS

Cake
1 3/4 cups vegetable oil
2 1/4 cups sugar
3 eggs
2 teaspoons Mexican vanilla extract
1 teaspoon almond extract
3 3/4 cups flour
1 1/2 teaspoons baking soda
1 1/2 teaspoons salt
1/3 teaspoon ground cinnamon
1 1/2 cups buttermilk
1 cup sweetened coconut flakes

Pineapple Filling
1 (8-ounce) piloncillo cone
1/3 cup granulated sugar
4 1/2 cups cubed fresh pineapple
2 Mexican cinnamon sticks
1/8 teaspoon salt
3/4 cup water, divided
2 1/2 tablespoons cornstarch

Buttercream Icing
1 cup butter, room temperature
3 cups confectioners' sugar
1 teaspoon Mexican vanilla extract
1/2 teaspoon almond extract
1/4 teaspoon salt
3 teaspoons heavy whipping cream

Toppings
1/2 cup pineapple juice
2 cups sweetened coconut flakes
small marshmallows for decoration
colored decorating sugar for decoration
small round candies for decoration

quickly until incorporated. Continue cooking for 3 minutes, until mixture thickens and glaze becomes clear.
4. Remove from heat and let cool to room temperature.

BUTTERCREAM ICING

1. Cream butter in a stand mixer on medium speed for 2 minutes. Add confectioners' sugar and mix until fully incorporated. Scrape bowl well, then mix on medium for an additional 1 minute.
2. Add vanilla, almond extract, and salt. Mix to fully combine. Scrape bowl down and add in whipping cream. Beat on medium-high for 3 minutes.
3. Place half the icing in a pastry bag fitted with a plain round tip. (I used a size 2A.)

ASSEMBLY

1. Remove cakes from pan and remove parchment paper. Cut the domed top off each cake with a serrated knife to create an even, flat surface. Using a pastry brush, brush the top of each cake with pineapple juice to moisten.
2. Place the first layer of cake on a cake stand. Pipe a lip of buttercream icing around the outer edge of the cake. Fill the inside of the buttercream lip with half the pineapple filling. Spread to create an even layer.
3. Place the next layer of cake on top and pipe a lip of buttercream icing around the outer edge of the cake. Fill the inside of the buttercream lip with the remaining pineapple filling. Spread to create an even layer.
4. Top with the last layer of cake. Press down slightly to make sure the cake is secure. Using an offset spatula, spread all remaining icing (including the set-aside portion and what remains in the piping bag) all over the outside of cake to cover the entire exterior. Smooth the buttercream by keeping the offset spatula flat and upright on the sides.
5. Pat shredded coconut evenly all around the edge of the cake, leaving the top layer of buttercream bare.
6. Cut marshmallows with sharp kitchen scissors diagonally. Dip sticky side of cut marshmallow into a dish of colored sugar to color marshmallow petals for marshmallow flowers. Decorate the the cake with colored marshmallow petals by placing dipped marshmallows on the cake colored side up. Place a small round candy in the center of each flower.
7. Refrigerate for 30 minutes minimum.

Berry *Pan Dulce* Cake

This snacking cake tastes like *pan dulce* with berries baked right in. It is the ideal cake to enjoy with a cup of *Café de Olla* (page 159) or *Chocolate Caliente de Agua* (page 160). Don't be fooled by its simplicity; it's packed with flavor. The sugar crust makes it extra cute.

Prep Time: 20 minutes   Bake Time: 1 hour 20 minutes   Yield: 10 servings

1. Preheat oven to 350 degrees.
2. Grease an 8-inch square metal cake pan with 1 tablespoon butter. Make sure to smear the butter all along the edge as well. Dust pan with 2 tablespoons sugar. Discard any excess sugar from the pan. Set pan to the side.
3. In a large mixer beat 1 cup sugar and remaining 6 tablespoons butter together until fluffy and pale yellow, 4 to 5 minutes. Add egg, crema Mexicana, and vanilla. Mix for another 3 to 4 minutes or until mixture comes together and is smooth.
4. In a separate bowl, sift flour and baking powder together. Slowly add flour mixture to butter mixture. Mix until incorporated.
5. Spoon mixture into prepared pan. With a rubber spatula, smooth the top evenly. Place strawberries along the edge of the cake to form an outside ring. Place cherries and blueberries in the middle. Sprinkle remaining 1 tablespoon sugar over the top of the berries.
6. Bake at 350 degrees for 15 minutes. Reduce heat to 325 degrees and bake for another 1 hour 5 minutes.
7. Allow cake to cool for 1 or 2 hours.

INGREDIENTS

7 tablespoons salted butter, room temperature, divided
1 cup plus 3 tablespoons sugar, divided
1 large egg
1/2 cup crema Mexicana or sour cream
1 teaspoon Mexican vanilla extract
1 1/2 cups flour
1 1/2 teaspoons baking powder
8 strawberries, cut in half lengthwise
8 fresh cherries, pitted
10 fresh blueberries

Cherry Tres Leches Cake

There is always room for Cherry Tres Leches Cake. Why would we have it any other way? The delicate fluffy cake is speckled with fresh cherry pieces and then drenched in cherry-laced three-milk liquid gold. Topped with homemade whipped cream and more cherries, this is the cake you give to the neighbors you really like.

Prep Time: 20 minutes   Bake Time: 35 minutes   Yield: 15 servings

CAKE

1. Preheat oven to 350 degrees. Spray a 9x13-inch glass baking dish with nonstick baking spray. Set to the side.
2. In a large bowl whisk flour, baking powder, and salt together. Add chopped cherries to flour mixture. Set to the side.
3. In a separate mixing bowl combine 3/4 cup sugar and egg yolks. Beat on high speed until combined and mixture is pale yellow. Add milk and vanilla and beat until well combined.
4. Pour egg mixture over flour mixture and mix with a rubber spatula until fully combined. Set to the side.
5. Add egg whites to an electric mixer with a whisk attachment and whip on high until slightly foamy and about to peak, about 2 minutes. Drizzle remaining 1/4 cup sugar over egg whites while the mixer is going. Whip until egg whites are stiff, about another 3 minutes.
6. Gently fold egg whites into flour mixture using a rubber spatula until combined. Do not overmix.
7. Pour batter into prepared baking dish and spread evenly. Bake for 35 minutes or until a toothpick comes out clean.
8. Let cake sit in pan for 15 minutes, then flip onto a platter.

INGREDIENTS

Cake
1 cup all-purpose flour
1 1/2 teaspoons baking powder
1/4 teaspoon sea salt
1/2 cup fresh cherries, pitted and quartered
1 cup sugar, divided
5 eggs, separated
1/3 cup milk
1 1/2 teaspoons Mexican vanilla extract

Tres Leches Cream
1 (14-ounce) can sweetened condensed milk
1 (12-ounce) can evaporated milk
1/3 cup half-and-half
1/2 cup fresh cherries, pitted and quartered

Toppings
whipped cream (page 102)
1 cup fresh cherries, pitted and quartered

TRES LECHES CREAM AND TOPPINGS

1. In a blender combine all tres leches cream ingredients. Blend until smooth.
2. Pierce the top of the cake with a fork many times for the tres leches cream to seep in. Very slowly pour tres leches cream on top of the cake, making sure to get the edges of the cake as well as the center. Allow the cake to sit until the cream is almost fully absorbed. There will be a little around the edge of the platter.
3. Once cake is fully cooled, top with homemade whipped cream and decorate with cherries. Enjoy!

Tip: To separate an egg means to divide the egg yolk from the egg white.
To do this, crack the shell without dropping the yolk. Transfer the yolk back and forth
between the eggshell halves, letting the egg white drip into a bowl,
then collecting the yolks in a separate bowl.

Cherry Carlota

Unlike the traditional lime Carlota, this one is loaded with cherries and takes on a beautiful lilac color. Not only is it a gorgeous dessert, it is also easy to make. This cake should be made a day before serving. Eat as is, or decorate with whipped cream on top for an extra-fancy occasion.

Prep Time: 20 minutes   Chill Time: 4 hours or overnight   Yield: 10 to 12 servings

1. Blend cherries, lime juice, sweetened condensed milk, and evaporated milk on high until cherries are completely puréed and mixture has a fluffy, thick consistency.
2. Spray a springform pan lightly with nonstick baking spray. Pour 1/2 cup cherry mixture into springform pan and spread to coat the bottom evenly.
3. Place cookies upright along the edge of the pan, then fill the bottom with a single layer of cookies.
4. Pour 1 cup cherry mixture over cookies. Continue to layer, alternating between cookies and cherry mixture, ending with the cherry mixture on top.
5. Refrigerate for at least 4 hours or preferably overnight.
6. Garnish with whipped cream, lime zest, cookies, and fresh cherries. Serve cold and enjoy!

INGREDIENTS

1 1/2 cups fresh cherries, pitted and stems removed, plus more for garnish
1/2 cup fresh lime juice, plus zest from peelings for garnish
2 (14-ounce) cans sweetened condensed milk
2 (12-ounce) cans evaporated milk
75 Marías cookies, plus more for garnish
whipped cream for garnish (page 102)

Peanut Butter Chocolate *Crepas Cake*

Layered cake is considered something special in my book. I know people make crepe cakes by stacking crepes on top of each other with gooey fillings in between, but never have I had a crepe cake with layers of crepes baked into the cake like this. It's a special treat. The peanut butter dulce de leche swirl frosting and fresh banana slices will seriously make you a firm believer in this unique cake.

Prep Time: 30 minutes   Bake Time: 35 minutes   Yield: 12 servings

CAKE

1. Preheat oven to 350 degrees. Spray 2 (8-inch) round cake pans with nonstick baking spray, then line the bottom of the pans with wax paper. Set to the side.
2. To prepare cinnamon tea, in a saucepan bring water and cinnamon sticks to a boil, then remove from heat and steep for 10 minutes. Allow to come to room temperature. Remove cinnamon sticks.
3. In a mixing bowl, combine flour, cocoa powder, baking soda, baking powder, and sugar. Add vegetable oil, eggs, vanilla, and buttermilk. Mix on medium for 2 minutes, then bring the speed up to medium-high for 2 more minutes. Pour in tea and mix until fully combined.
4. Pour 1/4 cup cake batter into the bottom of each prepared pan and spread evenly with a spatula. Top the thin layer of cake batter with a crepe. Pour another 1/4 cup batter on top and spread evenly, then top with another crepe. Continue layering cake batter and crepes until each pan has 5 crepes, then evenly distribute the remaining batter between both pans.
5. Bake for 30 to 35 minutes or until a toothpick inserted in the middle comes out clean.
6. Allow to cool completely. Remove cakes from their pans and remove the wax paper from the bottoms.

INGREDIENTS

10 crepes (page 109)

Cake Batter
1 cup water
2 Mexican cinnamon sticks
2 cups flour
1/2 cup cocoa powder, packed
1 teaspoon baking soda
1 teaspoon baking powder
2 cups sugar
1/2 cup vegetable oil
2 eggs
1 teaspoon Mexican vanilla extract
1 cup buttermilk

Frosting and Toppings
2 cups peanut butter
1 1/2 cups honey
2 bananas, sliced
3/4 cup dulce de leche (page 105)

1. In a bowl whisk peanut butter and honey together until completely combined. Spread half the peanut butter frosting on top of the first cake. Place sliced bananas on top of the peanut butter frosting. Place the second cake on top of the first. Spread remaining frosting on top of the second cake.
2. Swirl dulce de leche onto the top of the cake by making an indent in the frosting with the back of a spoon and filling the indents with dulce de leche. Cut and enjoy.

Tip: Cut crepes to fit perfectly to the size of the cake pan.

Choco-Horchata Cheesecake

Chocolate horchata cheesecake . . . Need I say more? You could lure me for a flight into outer space with a slice of this decadent cheesecake. The horchata and chocolate cookie flavor is not one you can purchase in a market and will become a fusion favorite for future generations.

Prep Time: 30 minutes   Cook Time: 1 hour   Cool Time: 1 hour 30 minutes   Chill Time: overnight   Yield: 12 servings

1. Preheat oven to 350 degrees. Spray a 9-inch springform pan with nonstick baking spray or grease with a generous amount of butter. Set to the side.
2. Boil several cups water, enough to fill a large glass baking dish halfway.

CRUST

1. Place cookies in a blender or food processor. Grind into a fine crumb. Add melted butter and mix until combined. The mixture should look like wet sand.
2. Press the cookie crumbs into the bottom of your prepared pan. Bake for 8 minutes to ensure a crisp crust.
3. Remove from oven and allow to cool while you make the filling.

FILLING

1. In a stand mixer beat cream cheese until smooth. Blend in all remaining filling ingredients except eggs. Whisk eggs in a separate bowl, then mix them into the cream cheese mixture until combined. Do not overmix.
2. Carefully wrap the bottom of the springform pan (with the crust still inside) with a few sheets of foil to ensure no water seeps into the pan from the water bath. Fold the sheets of foil over the top rim of the pan, careful not to get the aluminum inside the pan.
3. Pour the cheesecake filling over the cooled crust. Spread the top evenly with an offset knife. Tap the filled springform pan on the counter ten times to remove as many air bubbles as possible. Take a toothpick and further pop any little bubbles on the surface of the filling.

INGREDIENTS

Crust
1 package chocolate sandwich cookies (36 cookies)
4 tablespoons salted butter, melted

Filling
4 (8-ounce) bricks cream cheese, softened
1 cup sugar
1/2 cup brown sugar
1 1/2 teaspoons ground cinnamon
2/3 cup sour cream
1/3 cup horchata
1 teaspoon almond extract
4 eggs

Toppings
whipped cream (page 102)
1 teaspoon ground cinnamon

4. Transfer the foil-encased springform pan to a large baking dish. Fill the bottom of the baking dish with an inch of boiling hot water. The water bath will help reduce cracks in the cheesecake.
5. Bake for 1 hour. Turn off the oven and leave the cheesecake in the oven with the door closed for 30 minutes. Then crack the oven door 1 inch and leave the cheesecake in the oven to cool for an additional 1 hour.
6. Remove cheesecake from oven and water bath. Carefully unwrap pan. Run a butter knife around the edge of the cheesecake to loosen it slightly from the pan, but do not unmold yet. Place pan on a cooling rack and let cheesecake come completely to room temperature.
7. Place cheesecake, still in the pan and uncovered, in the fridge overnight to chill and set.

TOPPINGS

1. Run a butter knife around the edge of the cheesecake again once it is set and open the springform pan carefully.
2. Add whipped cream to a piping bag fitted with a tip and pipe whipped cream onto the cheesecake, creating the design of your choice. Sprinkle the top with ground cinnamon. Cut, serve, and enjoy!

Panadería
(Bakery)

Mazapán Donas

Filled donuts are nice, but they're not as nice as mazapán custard–filled donuts. This mazapán custard reminds the taste buds of what it is like to enjoy your favorite childhood candy stuffed in a fluffy donut. *Dee-licious!*

Prep Time: 25 minutes   Rest Time: 2 hours   Fry Time: 3 minutes per donut   Yield: 1 dozen large donuts or 30 mini donuts

DOUGH

1. Whisk milk, yeast, and sugar lightly in a medium-sized bowl. Set to the side for 10 minutes to allow yeast to foam.
2. Beat eggs, butter, and salt in a stand mixer fitted with the paddle attachment. Add yeast mixture and mix until combined.
3. Replace paddle attachment with dough hook attachment. Add half the flour and mix on medium speed until flour is combined, then add remaining flour and continue mixing until dough pulls away from mixing bowl, about 7 minutes total. Remove dough from mixer.
4. Transfer dough to a large greased bowl. Cover bowl with plastic wrap and allow dough to rise at room temperature for 1 hour or until dough doubles in size.
5. Roll dough out on a well-floured work surface to a 1/2-inch thickness. Cut into rounds using a circle cookie cutter or glass.
6. Place donut rounds on a floured surface and cover lightly with plastic wrap or a towel. Allow rounds to rise for 1 hour.

MAZAPÁN CUSTARD

1. Whisk egg yolks and sugar in a mixing bowl until sugar dissolves and mixture becomes pale yellow. Add salt and cornstarch and whisk until combined. Mixture will be thick.
2. Blend whipping cream, milk, and mazapán in a blender until completely combined. Pour milk into egg mixture and whisk until combined.
3. Strain mixture through a sieve into a heavy-bottomed pot. Cook on medium heat, stirring constantly, for 5 to 7 minutes or until mixture becomes a custard. Once custard has thickened, add vanilla.

INGREDIENTS

vegetable oil for frying

Dough
1 cup plus 2 tablespoons milk, warm (95 degrees)
2 heaping teaspoons active dry yeast
1/4 cup sugar
2 eggs
1/2 cup butter, melted and cooled
1/2 teaspoon salt
4 1/2 cups flour

Mazapán Custard
4 egg yolks
1/4 cup sugar
pinch of salt
1/4 cup cornstarch
3/4 cup heavy whipping cream
3/4 cup milk
2 mazapán candies
1/2 teaspoon Mexican vanilla extract

Chocolate Glaze
1/2 cup heavy whipping cream
3/4 cup chocolate chips

4. Remove custard from heat and transfer to a glass bowl. Cover with plastic wrap and allow to cool for 1 hour.

1. In a heavy-bottomed pot with a candy thermometer attached to the side, add 2 inches oil and heat to 375 degrees. Carefully add a few donuts at a time to the hot oil. Cook until golden brown, about 1 minutes 30 seconds on each side. Flip donuts with a slotted spoon or a long chopstick.
2. Transfer cooked donuts to a cooling rack. While the donut is still warm, take a chopstick and poke a hole on the side of each donut, making sure not to poke through the other side. Wiggle the chopstick a little to make room inside the donut.

1. Heat whipping cream in a saucepan over medium heat. Then stir in chocolate chips. Mix until chocolate melts and is smooth. Remove from heat and allow to cool for a few minutes.

1. Dip the top of each donut into chocolate glaze and allow it to dry and harden.
2. Place custard in a pastry bag with beveled tip for filling pastries. Insert the tip of the pastry bag into the side of the donut and squeeze to fill donut with custard. Eat immediately. (Old donuts never taste good.)

de la Rosa®

MAZAPÁN
ORIGINAL

peanut is nutritious   NO Artificial flavors   CONTAINS: 12 PIECES OF 1 OZ. EACH.   NET WT. 11.8 OZ (336g)

Churro Muffins

Churro muffins are officially the muffins of my dreams. These soft, moist muffins have speckles of cinnamon and butter in the center and a hard, crunchy, sweet top. They look like ordinary ol' muffins, but one bite in, you'll know that is far from the truth.

Prep Time: 30 minutes   Bake Time: 30 minutes per pan (2 pans)   Yield: 16 muffins

1. Preheat oven to 350 degrees. Line two cupcake pans with sixteen cupcake liners. Set to the side.

CINNAMON SUGAR

1. In a small mixing bowl, whisk sugar, cinnamon, and flour together. Cut in butter with your fingers. Set to the side.

CAKE

1. To prepare cinnamon tea, in a saucepan bring water and cinnamon sticks to a boil, then remove from heat and steep for 10 minutes. Allow to come to room temperature. Remove cinnamon stick.
2. In a stand mixer fitted with a whisk attachment, beat eggs and vegetable oil together on medium-high speed until completely combined and a bit thick, about 4 minutes. Pour in cinnamon tea, milk, and Mexican vanilla extract and mix for an additional 1 minute.
3. In a separate bowl mix flour, sugar, brown sugar, salt, baking powder, baking soda, and ground cinnamon together. Slowly pour dry ingredients into wet ingredients and mix until completely combined. Allow mixture to sit for 5 minutes.

ASSEMBLY

1. Fill each cupcake liner with 2 tablespoons batter. Crumble 1/2 teaspoon cinnamon sugar over each cupcake evenly with your fingers to create a center layer. Top with 2 more heaping tablespoons cake batter. Sprinkle each top with 1/2 teaspoon turbinado sugar.
2. Bake for 30 to 35 minutes or until toothpick inserted in the middle comes out clean.

Tip: Make cinnamon tea (step 3) before you start making this recipe. Allow it to come to room temperature.

INGREDIENTS

Cinnamon Sugar
1/2 cup sugar
1 tablespoon ground cinnamon
1/4 cup flour
4 tablespoons butter, room temperature

Cake
1/2 cup water
1 Mexican cinnamon stick
3 eggs
1 1/4 cups vegetable oil
1 1/4 cups milk
1 teaspoon Mexican vanilla extract
2 cups flour
1 cup sugar
3/4 cup brown sugar
1 teaspoon salt
1 teaspoon baking powder
1 teaspoon baking soda
1 teaspoon ground cinnamon

Topping
8 teaspoons turbinado sugar

Bisquets

Bury me in *bisquets*! These buttery sweet biscuits play really nicely with raspberry jam or a champagne marmalade. They are the guest of honor at any tea party. Don't be surprised if they make your invitees squeal with delight; they carry that kind of charm.

Prep Time: 30 minutes   Chill Time: 1 hour   Bake Time: 20 minutes per baking sheet (2 baking sheets)   Yield: 16 bisquets

1. Lightly grease two baking sheets or line them with parchment paper. Set to the side.
2. Whisk flour, sugar, salt, baking powder, and baking soda together in a large mixing bowl. Incorporate grated butter into flour mixture with your fingers. You are looking for pea-sized balls of butter.
3. Add eggs and buttermilk. Mix with hands until combined and dough comes together.
4. On a floured work surface, roll out dough to a 1-inch thickness. Then fold both ends toward the center; it should look like the beginning of a paper airplane. Take the right-hand fold and fold it over the left side. Then reroll the dough to a 1-inch thickness. Cut dough using a 3-inch round cutter. Reroll scraps and continue cutting until all dough is used.
5. Place on prepared baking sheets 2 inches apart. Take a 1-inch round cutter and indent the middle of each *bisquet* top, not pushing all the way through.
6. Chill in the refrigerator for 1 hour.
7. Preheat oven to 375 degrees.
8. Whisk all egg wash ingredients together in a small bowl. Brush *bisquets* with glossy egg wash.
9. Bake for 15 to 20 minutes or until golden brown.
10. Serve with jam, butter, and cream cheese.

INGREDIENTS

6 cups flour
1/2 cup sugar
1 teaspoon salt
2 1/2 tablespoons baking powder
1 teaspoon baking soda
1 3/4 cups salted butter, frozen and grated
2 eggs
1 3/4 cups buttermilk

Glossy Egg Wash
1 egg
1/16 teaspoon salt
1/16 teaspoon sugar

Funfetti *Conchas*

FUN-fetti *conchas*! Not only are they magic in the mouth, they are easy on the eyes too with just the right amount of color. This is a sweet spin on the widely known dome-shaped Mexican classic sweet bread. Add a few tablespoons of Funfetti and turn everyday *conchas* into celebrational ones perfect for a *cumpleaños* (birthday).

Prep Time: 30 minutes   Rest Time: 3 hours   Bake Time: 20 minutes per pan (2 pans)   Yield: 8 conchas

DOUGH

1. In a small bowl combine yeast, 1/2 teaspoon sugar, and warm water together to activate yeast. Mix to combine and allow to get frothy, about 10 minutes. Set to the side.
2. In a stand mixer fitted with the whisk attachment, whisk together bread flour, salt, and remaining 1/2 cup plus 2 tablespoons sugar. Change the attachment to a dough hook and add butter. Mix until butter is incorporated and forms pea-sized balls.
3. Add eggs and vanilla. Mix until incorporated. The dough will look shaggy and a bit floury still.
4. *Add activated yeast. Mix with dough hook on* medium for about 10 minutes. The dough will be soft and pull easily.
5. Remove dough from mixer and place on a floured surface. Knead for 1 or 2 minutes and shape into a ball. Place in greased bowl, cover with plastic wrap, and set in a warm place (80 to 85 degrees). Let dough double in size for 2 hours.
6. Once dough has doubled in size, divide it into 8 even pieces. Weigh them if you have a scale. If not, try and make them as uniform as possible.
7. Grease two baking sheets and your hands. Roll each piece of dough into a ball and flatten slightly between the hands to make a thick round disk. Rub a little grease on the top of each dough disk, then place on prepared baking sheets.
8. Once all dough is shaped, set in a warm place to double in size, about 1 hour.

INGREDIENTS

Dough
3 teaspoons active dry yeast
1/2 cup plus 2 tablespoons plus 1/2 teaspoon baker's sugar, divided
1/2 cup warm water (between 100 and 110 degrees)
3 3/4 cups bread flour
1/2 teaspoon salt
1/2 cup butter, room temperature
2 eggs
1 teaspoon Mexican vanilla extract

Concha Topping
1/2 cup vegetable shortening
1/2 cup confectioners' sugar
1 cup all-purpose flour
3 tablespoons Funfetti sprinkles, plus more for sprinkling

TOPPING

1. In a stand mixer fitted with the paddle attachment, add shortening and confectioners' sugar. Mix until combined.
2. Slowly pour in flour until completely combined. If the mixture does not come together easily when done, add flour a tablespoon at a time until the mixture becomes like paste.
3. Add Funfetti sprinkles and mix until combined.

ASSEMBLY

1. Preheat oven to 325 degrees.
2. With floured hands, roll 1 tablespoon topping into a ball. Make 8 balls total. Line a tortilla press with floured parchment paper or a plastic bag. Place each topping ball in the middle and press down to make a flattened disk. Carefully remove disk from press and place on top of *concha*. Repeat until all *conchas* are covered.
3. Score *concha* topping with a paring knife to create decorative lines. Sprinkle with more Funfetti.
4. Bake for 20 minutes or until golden on the bottom.
5. Remove from oven and let cool 10 minutes on the baking sheet. Place on a cooling rack, let come to room temperature, and enjoy!

Dulcería
(Sweets)

Perfect Whipped Cream

Whipped cream is the easiest thing to make and elevates many desserts in the simplest way. This is my way to whip up a batch. It's not too sweet and is perfectly creamy.

Freeze Time: 30 minutes   *Prep Time: 5 minutes*   *Yield: 1 cup*

1. Freeze the bowl of a stand mixer for 30 minutes.
2. Attach frozen bowl to a stand mixer fitted with whisk attachment.
3. Add whipping cream and whisk on high until soft peaks form, about 2 minutes 30 seconds.
4. Sprinkle in sugar and whisk until stiff peaks form, about 2 minutes more.

> *Tip: Always look for the highest fat content on whipping cream.*

> *Tip: Freezing the mixing bowl and using super-cold whipping cream helps the whipping cream form into peaks faster.*

INGREDIENTS

1 cup heavy whipping cream
1/4 cup sugar

Dulce de Leche

Have you ever tasted a fresh batch of dulce de leche right out of the can? This is a super easy semi-homemade method. I like to keep some in the fridge and use it when the occasion calls. Sometimes it's just a spoonful and I am satisfied.

Prep Time: 5 minutes   *Cook Time: 3 hours 30 minutes*   *Cool Time: overnight*   *Yield: 1 3/4 cups*

1. Place unopened can of sweetened condensed milk in a stockpot. Cover with water by several inches. Bring water to a boil.
2. Once boiling, cover pot with a lid and reduce heat to medium. Cook for 3 hours 30 minutes, replenishing the hot water every 45 minutes to ensure can is covered by several inches of water at all times.
3. Remove pot from heat and leave can in hot water. Allow water and can to come to room temperature for several hours or overnight.
4. Once can has cooled completely, remove from water. Open and scoop out dulce de leche. Place in a jar and store in the fridge. It will keep for 2 weeks.

Tip: Here's a tip for drizzling. Mix 4 heaping tablespoons cold dulce de leche and 1 tablespoon water in a small saucepan over medium-low heat. The dulce de leche will become fluid and easy to drizzle.

INGREDIENTS

1 (14-ounce) can sweetened condensed milk

Strawberry Churro Bites

These strawberry churro bites are perfectly infused with a hint of strawberry in the batter and further enhanced with *fresa* flavor by dipping them in a strawberry glaze. Pour them in a cup to enjoy at a gathering or for family movie night. Serve with fresh strawberries for a balance between sweet dough bites and a little bit of mother nature.

Prep Time: 25 minutes   **Cook Time: 30 minutes**   **Yield: 6 cups churro bites**

BATTER

1. Mash strawberries with a masher, then strain them through a sieve. Reserve 4 tablespoons strawberry purée for strawberry glaze.
2. In a small saucepan combine 1/2 cup strawberry purée, water, sugar, and butter over medium heat. Bring mixture to a boil and quickly remove from heat.
3. Stir in flour with a rubber spatula until mixture forms a ball. Place in a stand mixer and allow to cool for 10 minutes.
4. Add eggs and mix for a few minutes until mixture comes together. Set to the side.

CINNAMON SUGAR

1. Mix cinnamon sugar ingredients together in a bowl. Set to the side.

FRYING

1. Heat oil in a deep frying pot fitted with a candy thermometer. Bring the temperature to 375 degrees. Line a plate with paper towels.
2. Pour dough into a piping bag with a large star tip (size 1M). Pipe dough in desired shape (about 1 inch long) into hot oil. Fry until golden, about 2 minutes. Remove from oil using a slotted spoon and drain on prepared plate for a few minutes. Roll warm churro bites in cinnamon sugar until completely coated. Repeat with remaining dough.

STRAWBERRY GLAZE

1. In a small mixing bowl whisk confectioners' sugar and reserved 4 tablespoons strawberry purée together. Glaze will be slightly thick. Pour into little dipping bowls.
2. Serve churros with strawberry glaze and fresh strawberries!

Tip: Squeeze out long churro strips and cut them into 1-inch pieces with scissors before frying. Or leave churro strips long and fry for 3 to 4 minutes or until golden brown (page 100-101).

INGREDIENTS

6 cups vegetable oil for frying

Batter
15 fresh strawberries, plus more for serving
1 1/2 cups water
1/4 cup sugar
6 tablespoons salted butter
2 1/4 cups flour
2 eggs

Cinnamon Sugar
1/4 cup sugar
1/2 teaspoon ground cinnamon

Strawberry Glaze
2 cups confectioners' sugar
4 tablespoons strawberry purée (see step 1)

Mexican *Crepas con Mango*

Most people know these ultrathin pancakes as crepes. In Mexico they are referred to as *crepas*! I prepare them and fill the center with sweet mangoes or whatever seasonal fruit I have on hand for a quick dessert. They are super versatile and can be filled with Nutella, pudding, or whipped cream. I also use them to make my Peanut Butter Chocolate *Crepas* Cake (page 78).

Prep Time: 10 minutes   Chill Time: 1 hour   Cook Time: 2 minutes per crepe   Yield: 10 crepes

1. Combine all crepe ingredients in a blender until smooth. Refrigerate batter for 1 hour.
2. Heat a greased nonstick skillet over medium heat. Lift skillet and add 1/4 cup batter. Tilt skillet in a circular motion to make a perfectly round crepe. Place back on stove and cook for 1 minute. Flip crepe and cook on other side for 45 seconds or until slightly browned. Remove from pan. Repeat until all batter is used.
3. Fill with sliced mango (or any fruit of your choice) and a drizzle of sweetened condensed milk. Fold in quarters.

   Tip: Grease pan with a dab of butter or nonstick cooking spray.

INGREDIENTS

Crepes
1 cup flour, sifted
1 1/3 cups milk
2 eggs
2 tablespoons sugar
1 teaspoon Mexican vanilla extract
1 teaspoon vegetable oil
1/8 teaspoon salt

Filling
sliced mango
sweetened condensed milk

Limas de Coco

I like to think of *Limas de Coco* as bite-size gems. The lime and coconut swirl together in a decadent dance for the mouth. These treats can be made in advance and kept in an airtight container for up to a week.

Prep Time: 15 minutes   Cook Time: 4 hours plus 10 minutes   Cool Time: 2 hours plus overnight   Yield: 10 limes

INGREDIENTS

lots of water for boiling

3 teaspoons baking soda, divided

10 medium limes, rinsed well

3 cups granulated sugar, divided

1 1/4 cups sweetened coconut flakes

1/4 cup water

1. Boil 8 cups water and 1 teaspoon baking soda in a large pot. Once water is boiling, add limes. Reduce heat to medium and cook for 30 minutes, until tender. Strain and allow limes to cool.
2. Once you are able to handle the limes with your hands, take a paring knife and make a small incision at the top of each lime. Try to keep the incision as small as you can and avoid tearing the rind. Carefully remove the inside lime flesh by scraping it out with the paring knife or a tiny spoon. Discard lime flesh.
3. In the same pot bring 8 cups water and remaining 2 teaspoons baking soda to a boil. Add empty lime rinds. Boil for 30 minutes. Strain.
4. Refill pot with enough cold water to cover lime rinds. Do not add baking soda. Bring to a boil. Strain. Repeat the process in this step 4 more times (5 times without baking soda total). This process will remove the bitter taste from the rinds and prime them to become candied.
5. After straining water the fifth time, refill with enough cold water to cover lime rinds. Add 2 1/2 cups sugar and mix to combine. Cook over medium heat for 20 to 25 minutes to create a syrup.
6. Turn heat off and allow limes to cool in liquid for 2 hours.
7. Remove lime rinds and place on a cooling rack to drip-dry for a minimum of 8 hours or overnight.
8. In a small saucepan over medium heat, combine remaining 1/2 cup sugar, coconut, and 1/4 cup water. Cook for 10 minutes or until liquid is absorbed. Remove from heat and transfer to a bowl to cool completely.
9. Fill each lime rind with 2 tablespoons coconut. Shape with hands to make sure coconut is compact. Bite into the lime and enjoy!

Gelatinas
(Gelatin)

Lime Vanilla *Flotatina* (Floating Gelatin)

Even though this *gelatina* is named "Lime Vanilla Flotatina," I feel like it should have a name along the lines of something more bewitching, like "Mischievous Floating Fairy Gelatin." This blissful light-as-a-feather dessert is definitely a beautiful balance between creamy and fruity. I used lime gelatin for this recipe, but it is interchangeable with strawberry, delivering the same amount of pizzazz.

Prep Time: 30 minutes   Chill Time: 12 hours or overnight plus 30 minutes   Yield: 10 to 12 servings

1. Spray a 12-cup Bundt pan with nonstick cooking spray. Set to the side.

VANILLA CREAM LAYER

1. Dissolve unflavored gelatin in hot water. Stir until gelatin fully dissolves.
2. Blend dissolved gelatin, cream cheese, sweetened condensed milk, evaporated milk, and vanilla to create vanilla cream.
3. Pour vanilla cream into prepared Bundt pan. Refrigerate for a minimum of 4 hours to firm.

LIME LAYER I

1. Mix 3 1/2 teaspoons unflavored gelatin, 1 box lime gelatin, and 2 cups hot water until completely combined. Then mix in 2 cups cold water. Allow to come to room temperature.
2. Remove vanilla cream gelatin from fridge. Carefully pull gelatin away from all edges with your fingers. Create a space between the wall of the mold and the vanilla cream gelatin by holding it with your fingers. Carefully pour lime gelatin into the side space. Vanilla cream gelatin should float on top of lime gelatin. If it is not floating on its own, run a butter knife around the edge; this should lift it into place.
3. Refrigerate for 4 hours.

INGREDIENTS

Vanilla Cream Layer
2 (0.25-ounce) packets unflavored gelatin
1/2 cup boiling hot water
1 (8-ounce) brick cream cheese, room temperature
1 (14-ounce) can sweetened condensed milk
1 (12-ounce) can evaporated milk
1 teaspoon Mexican vanilla extract

Lime Layers
2 (0.25-ounce) packets unflavored gelatin, divided
2 (6 ounce) boxes lime gelatin, divided
3 cups boiling hot water, divided
3 cups cold water, divided

1. Mix remaining 1 1/2 teaspoons unflavored gelatin, remaining 1 box lime gelatin, and remaining 1 cup hot water until completely combined. Then mix in remaining 1 cup cold water. Allow to come to room temperature.
2. Remove gelatin from fridge and pour final lime mixture over the top. Refrigerate for 4 hours or overnight.

UNMOLDING

1. With both hands gently pull gelatin away from the wall of the Bundt pan. Work all the way around little by little. Don't forget the center.
2. Fill a big bowl with warm to hot water. Slowly glide the pan into the water bath. Let it rest there for 10 to 15 seconds. You will see the insides of the pan become slightly moist; this is the sign you are looking for. Remove pan from water and dry with a towel.
3. Place a plate on top of the pan and flip it over. You will hear a plop. Gently remove pan. You will have a beautiful and delicious gelatin.
4. Refrigerate for 30 minutes to allow it to firm up again.

Banana Split Mosaic *Gelatina*

This *gelatina* embodies all the favorite banana split flavors (vanilla, chocolate, strawberry, and banana) under one mold. Top it with a dollop of whipped cream, some chopped peanuts, and a maraschino cherry for a jiggly wiggly *bananas* experience.

Prep Time: 30 minutes   Chill Time: 3 hours, 8 hours or overnight, and 30 minutes   Yield: 10 to 12 servings

CHOCOLATE GELATIN

1. Sprinkle unflavored gelatin in hot water and mix to dissolve. Set to the side.
2. Heat sweetened condensed milk and evaporated milk over low heat. When mixture starts to boil, mix in chocolate chips and stir until smooth.
3. Remove from heat. Stir in unflavored gelatin mixture until completely incorporated.
4. Spray a 2-quart glass baking dish with nonstick cooking spray. Pour in chocolate gelatin. Refrigerate for 3 hours or until firm.

BANANA GELATIN

1. Sprinkle unflavored gelatin in hot water and mix to dissolve. Set to the side.
2. Blend sweetened condensed milk, evaporated milk, bananas, sugar, and vanilla until smooth. Add food coloring, if desired.
3. Add unflavored gelatin mixture and blend again to incorporate.
4. Spray a 2-quart glass baking dish with nonstick cooking spray. Pour in banana gelatin. Refrigerate for 3 hours or until firm.

STRAWBERRY GELATIN

1. Mix strawberry gelatin powder and hot water together until completely dissolved.
2. Spray a 2-quart glass baking dish with nonstick cooking spray. Pour in strawberry gelatin. Refrigerate for 3 hours or until firm.

INGREDIENTS

Chocolate Gelatin
2 (0.25-ounce) packets unflavored gelatin
3/4 cup boiling hot water
1/2 cup sweetened condensed milk
1 cup evaporated milk
1 (12-ounce) bag chocolate chips

Banana Gelatin
2 (0.25-ounce) packets unflavored gelatin
3/4 cup boiling hot water
1/2 cup sweetened condensed milk
1 cup evaporated milk
2 ripe bananas
1/2 cup sugar
1 teaspoon Mexican vanilla extract
yellow gel food coloring (optional)

Strawberry Gelatin
2 (6-ounce) packets strawberry gelatin
2 3/4 cups boiling hot water

Vanilla Gelatin
4 (0.25-ounce) packets unflavored gelatin
3/4 cup boiling hot water
1 (14-ounce) can sweetened condensed milk
1 (12-ounce) can evaporated milk
2 cups milk
1/2 cup sugar
1 teaspoon Mexican vanilla extract
1 cup mini marshmallows

Toppings
whipped cream (page 102)
chopped peanuts
maraschino cherries

VANILLA GELATIN

1. Begin vanilla gelatin 45 minutes before other gelatins finish. Sprinkle unflavored gelatin in hot water and mix to dissolve. Set to the side.
2. Heat remaining vanilla gelatin ingredients except marshmallows over low heat until sugar dissolves.
3. Remove from heat. Stir in unflavored gelatin mixture until completely incorporated.
4. Pour 1 cup vanilla gelatin mixture in a lightly greased 12-cup Bundt pan. Sprinkle in mini marshmallows. Refrigerate for 30 minutes.

ASSEMBLY

1. Cut chocolate, banana, and strawberry gelatin into squares. Place cubes in Bundt pan over vanilla gelatin. Pour remaining vanilla gelatin mixture over gelatin cubes. Refrigerate for 8 hours or overnight.

UNMOLDING

1. With both hands gently pull gelatin away from the wall of the Bundt pan. Work all the way around little by little. Don't forget the center.
2. Fill a big bowl with warm to hot water. Slowly glide the pan into the water bath. Let it rest there for 10 to 15 seconds. You will see the insides of the pan become slightly moist; this is the sign you are looking for. Remove pan from water and dry with a towel.
3. Place a plate on top of the pan and flip it over. You will hear a plop. Gently remove pan. You will have a beautiful and delicious gelatin.
4. Refrigerate for 30 minutes to allow it to firm up again.
5. Top with whipped cream, chopped peanuts, and a cherry.

Gelatina Arco Iris (Rainbow Gelatin)

This dreamy-looking rainbow *gelatina* can stand on its own as the centerpiece on any table. It also doubles as a gorgeous homage to Pride Month. They say there is an enchanted land at the end of every rainbow . . . hopefully you feel lucky your first bite in.

Prep Time: 30 minutes   Chill Time: 4 hours, overnight, and 30 minutes   Yield: 10 to 12 servings

MILKY LAYERS

1. Place 1/4 cup red gelatin mix in its own bowl. Set remaining red gelatin powder to the side. Repeat with remaining colors. Colors will remain separate.
2. Add 1 teaspoon unflavored gelatin to each bowl. Mix to combine.
3. Add 2/3 cup boiling hot water to each bowl. Mix until gelatin is completely dissolved.
4. Add 1/3 cup sweetened condensed milk to each bowl. Mix well. Set to the side.

NON-MILKY LAYERS

1. Place remaining red gelatin mix (a little over 1/2 cup) in its own bowl. Repeat with remaining colors.
2. Add 1/2 teaspoon unflavored gelatin to each bowl. Mix to combine.
3. Add 1 cup boiling hot water to each bowl. Mix until gelatin is completely dissolved. Set to the side.

ASSEMBLY

1. Spray a 12-cup Bundt pan with nonstick cooking spray.
2. Choose the order you want your colors to stack in, alternating between milky layers and non-milky layers.
3. Pour first color (milky or non-milky layer only, not both) in prepared pan. Refrigerate for 30 minutes.

INGREDIENTS

6 (6-ounce) boxes gelatin mix (red, orange, yellow, green, blue, purple)
4 (0.25-ounce) packets unflavored gelatin
10 cups boiling hot water
2 (14-ounce) cans sweetened condensed milk

4. Gently pour in next layer. Refrigerate for 20 minutes. Repeat until all layers have been added.
5. Let gelatin set overnight.

UNMOLDING

1. With both hands, gently pull gelatin away from the wall of the Bundt pan. Work all the way around little by little. Don't forget the center.
2. Fill a big bowl with warm to hot water. Slowly glide the pan into the water bath. Let it rest there for 10 to 15 seconds. You will see the insides of the pan become slightly moist; this is the sign you are looking for. Remove pan from water and dry with a towel.
3. Place a plate on top of the pan and flip it over. You will hear a plop. Gently remove pan. You will have a beautiful and delicious gelatin.
4. Refrigerate for 30 minutes to allow it to firm up again.

Tip: You will know a layer is done by pressing on the top. If your fingerprint remains, you are safe to add the next layer.

Tip: While the first layer chills, let other layers come to room temperature. The first layer, which will be warmer than the others, will take 30 minutes to firm up, but layers added at room temperature will take only 20 minutes.

Arroz con Leche
(Rice Pudding)

Arroz con Leche Brûlée

This extravagant version of *arroz con leche* is so creamy and decadent, in the same vein as crème brûlée, that I was led to imagine my *arroz con leche* topped with a layer of hardened caramelized sugar and adorned with fresh fruit. It's a fusion of two desserts elevated to new heights! The addition of the pecans and the toasty bits the torch creates while melting the sugar are all welcome textures to this dessert. I can't even explain how absolutely delicious it is.

Prep Time: 10 minutes   Cook Time: 40 minutes   Yield: 6 bowls

1. Boil water, vanilla, and cinnamon stick in a heavy-bottomed pot over high heat.
2. Add rice and mix to distribute evenly. Lower heat and simmer 20 to 25 minutes or until water evaporates.
3. Whisk sweetened condensed milk and half-and-half together in a separate bowl. Add to cooked rice. Cook on medium-high for an additional 10 to 15 minutes to thicken, stirring occasionally so the mixture does not stick to the bottom of pot and so the milk doesn't burn.
4. Remove from heat. Remove cinnamon stick with a pair of tongs. Mix in chopped pecans.
5. Divide equally into 6 bowls. Sprinkle the top of each bowl with 1 1/2 heaping tablespoons sugar. Using a torch, melt sugar to form a crispy top. Cool 5 minutes.
6. Decorate with fresh fruit and enjoy!

INGREDIENTS

3 1/2 cups water
1 teaspoon Mexican vanilla extract
1 Mexican cinnamon stick
1 cup short-grain rice
1 (14-ounce) can sweetened condensed milk
1 cup half-and-half
1/3 cup chopped candied pecans (optional)
9 heaping tablespoons granulated sugar
fruit for garnish

Toasted Pine Nut and Fig *Arroz con Leche*

Pine nuts and figs . . . oh my! The toasted pine nuts couple flawlessly with the figs, and jasmine rice is the secret component adding an extra wink of sweetness to this *arroz con leche*. It's one big flavor party!

Prep Time: 10 minutes   Cook Time: 45 minutes   Yield: 6 servings

ARROZ CON LECHE

1. Boil water and cinnamon sticks in a pot over medium-high heat. Once water is boiling, remove cinnamon sticks.
2. Pour jasmine rice into boiling water. Mix to combine. Cover, then simmer on low for 20 minutes.
3. Remove lid and add vanilla, sweetened condensed milk, and evaporated milk. Mix well to combine. Cook, uncovered, on medium-high for an additional 5 minutes, stirring occasionally.
4. Remove from heat and cool 10 minutes.

PINE NUTS

1. Preheat toaster oven to 350 degrees. Line a small baking tray with aluminum foil.
2. Spread pine nuts evenly on baking tray. Bake 5 to 7 minutes or until they start to brown and become fragrant.
3. Remove from oven. Sprinkle with confectioners' sugar while still hot. Mix to coat all nuts evenly.

ASSEMBLY

1. Serve *arroz con leche* warm. Garnish with toasted pine nuts and figs. Enjoy!

INGREDIENTS

Arroz con Leche
4 cups water
2 Mexican cinnamon sticks
1 3/4 cups jasmine rice
1 teaspoon Mexican vanilla extract
1 (14-ounce) can sweetened condensed milk
1 (12-ounce) can evaporated milk
fresh figs for garnish

Pine Nuts
1/2 cup pine nuts
2 tablespoons confectioners' sugar

Días Festivos
(Holidays)

Día de los Muertos Conchas

These *calavera* (skull) *conchas* came to me in a dream. I was setting up my altar for *Día de los Muertos* and kept saying I wanted something that would pop. A voice with no face suggested *conchas*. I'm not sure if it was a subconscious element that suggested *conchas*—since that is what my grandfather used to eat with his coffee— or if it was my grandfather paying me a visit in dream form, but I woke up and knew I had to bring them to life. I hope you will have fun making these cute *conchas* and let them pop on your altar . . . not to mention they are absolutely delicious for the living to eat!

Prep Time: 30 minutes   Rest Time: 3 to 4 hours   Bake Time: 20 minutes   Yield: 1 dozen conchas

DOUGH

1. In a small bowl combine yeast, 1 tablespoon sugar, and warm milk together to activate yeast. Mix to combine and allow to get frothy, about 10 minutes.
2. In a stand mixer fitted with the whisk attachment, add bread flour, remaining 3/4 cup sugar, and salt and whisk together. Change the attachment to a dough hook and add butter. Mix until butter is incorporated and forms pea-sized balls.
3. Add eggs and vanilla. Mix until incorporated. The dough will look shaggy and a bit floury still.
4. Add activated yeast. Mix with dough hook on medium for about 10 minutes. The dough will be soft and pull easily.
5. Remove dough from mixer and place on a floured surface. Knead for 1 to 2 minutes and shape into a ball. Place in greased bowl, cover with plastic wrap, and set in a warm place (80 to 85 degrees). Let dough double in size for 2 hours.
6. Once dough has doubled in size, divide it into 12 even pieces. Weigh them if you have a scale. If not, try and make them as uniform as possible.
7. Grease two baking sheets and your hands. Roll each piece of dough into a ball and flatten slightly between the hands to make a thick, round disk. Rub a little grease on the top of each dough disk, then place on prepared baking sheets.

INGREDIENTS

Dough
4 1/2 teaspoons active dry yeast
3/4 cup plus 1 tablespoon baker's sugar, divided
3/4 cup milk, warm (between 100 and 110 degrees)
4 cups bread flour
1/2 teaspoon salt
1/2 cup butter, room temperature
4 eggs
1 teaspoon Mexican vanilla extract

Concha Topping
3/4 cup vegetable shortening
3/4 cup confectioners' sugar
1 1/2 cups all-purpose flour
gel food coloring of your choice

8. Once all dough is shaped, set in a warm place to double in size, for 1 to 2 hours.

TOPPING

1. In a stand mixer fitted with the paddle attachment, add shortening and confectioners' sugar. Mix until combined. Slowly pour in flour until completely combined. If the mixture does not come together easily when done, add flour a tablespoon at a time until the mixture becomes like paste.
2. Set aside at least 12 tablespoons topping to be the white base of the calavera decoration. Dye the remaining topping with food coloring as you'd like.

ASSEMBLY

1. Preheat oven to 325 degrees.
2. With floured hands, roll 1 tablespoon white topping into a ball. Make 12 balls total. Line a tortilla press with floured parchment paper or a plastic bag. Place each topping ball in the middle and press down to make a flattened disk. Carefully remove disk from press and place on top of *concha*. Repeat until all conchas are covered.
3. Score *concha* topping with a paring knife to create decorative lines.
4. Decorate as you wish with the remaining colors of *concha* topping.
5. Bake for 20 minutes or until golden on the bottom.
6. Remove from oven and let cool 10 minutes on the baking sheet. Place on a cooling rack, let come to room temperature, and enjoy!

Tip: I doubled the topping recipe and left half white and dyed the other half. I treated the colors as I would play dough and did all the shaping with my hands. I made little upside-down hearts for noses, petal-like shapes for teeth, crosses for head adornments, and round eyes in various colors. You can make your conchas as ornate as you'd like or keep them simple. I used a toothpick for finer detail shaping.

Individual *Pan de Muertos*

Pan de muerto is eaten in celebration of the dearly departed on and leading up to *Día de los Muertos*. They come in different sizes and flavors and are placed on the altar as an offering for the dead. These small *pan de muertos* are perfect for a smaller altar or to eat with a mug of Cinnamon *Atole* (page 156).

Prep Time: 25 minutes   **Rest Time: 2 hours**   **Bake Time: 25 minutes**   **Yield: 6 individual loaves**

1. Combine yeast, 1/4 cup sugar, and milk and mix until smooth. Cover with a kitchen towel and let rest at room temperature for 10 minutes or until foamy.
2. Place yeast mixture in a stand mixer fitted with the dough attachment. Add eggs and yolks one by one until fully mixed in.
3. In a separate bowl mix flour, salt, and remaining 3/4 cup sugar. Add dry ingredients to wet ingredients and mix until you get a smooth dough.
4. Add butter, orange blossom water, orange zest, and anise seed. Mix until dough is smooth and elastic.
5. Remove dough from mixer and shape into a ball. Place in a lightly greased bowl, cover with plastic wrap, and let rise for 1 hour or until doubled in size.
6. Set dough on a floured work surface, punch it down, and divide it into 4 equal portions. Set 1 portion to the side; it will be used to form the heads and bones.
7. Divide each of the remaining 3 portions in half. Roll the 6 portions of dough into balls again, then place on a greased tray and flatten lightly. These will be the buns.
8. To form the head and bones of the bread, take the reserved large portion of dough and divide it into 24 small dough balls. Of the 24 small dough balls, set 6 to the side; these will be the head knobs.
9. Take 1 of the remaining 18 balls and roll it up and down with 3 fingers to divide it into 4 parts without cutting it completely. It will look like a long 4-part worm. Do the same with the 17 remaining small dough balls. These will be the bones.

INGREDIENTS

2 tablespoons active dry yeast
1 cup sugar, divided
1 1/2 cups milk, warm (between 100 and 110 degrees)
4 whole eggs plus 3 egg yolks
8 cups flour
1/2 tablespoon salt
1 cup butter, cubed, room temperature
1 tablespoon orange blossom water
zest of 1 orange
1 teaspoon anise seed
sesame seeds for garnish

10. Brush each of the 6 large reserved portions of dough on the greased baking sheet with a little water. Stretch one of the bones and place it on one of the buns, covering it from side to side. Place a second bone perpendicular to the first to crisscross the bones. Then place a third bone down the middle of the two crossed bones. Glaze one of the small head-knob dough spheres with a little water and place it on top of the intersection of all the bones. Repeat this step with the rest of the buns, bones, and spheres.
11. Sprinkle buns with sesame seeds. Let loaves rise for 1 hour or until doubled in size.
12. Preheat oven to 350 degrees. Bake loaves for 25 minutes or until golden brown. Let cool on a cooling rack.

Tip: Orange blossom water can be bought from specialty gourmet markets or online. The key to flavoring the dough with orange blossom water is to not overdo it. One tablespoon adds the perfect hint of orange to the dough.

Calabaza en Tacha (Spiced Candied Pumpkin)

Calabaza en tacha is typically enjoyed in the days leading up to *Día de los Muertos*, but it is also enjoyed as a sweet breakfast or dessert throughout the fall season. In Mexico, *calabaza de castilla*—a type of winter squash, of the species *Cucurbita moschata*—is used for this dish and takes longer to cook. In the United States, I use a small pie pumpkin (a pumpkin grown for cooking rather than for decoration or carving) and reduce the cooking time. Cooked in a piloncillo syrup and perfectly spiced, this old-fashioned recipe is one that will never die.

Prep Time: 10 minutes   Cook Time: 1 hour   Yield: 6 servings

1. Cut pumpkin by removing the stem first. Cut down the middle and scoop out the seeds. Slice into 2-inch-wide slices. Set to the side.
2. In a big stockpot over medium-high heat, add all remaining pumpkin ingredients. Bring to a boil and allow piloncillo to melt, stirring occasionally.
3. Once syrup is boiling, add in pumpkin slices. Cover and reduce heat to low. Cook for 1 hour or until fork-tender.
4. Place candied pumpkin slices on a plate and drizzle with syrup and a little milk or whipping cream, if desired. Enjoy warm.

   Tip: Traditionally people eat calabaza en tacha *in a bowl of milk. I prefer to use whipping cream for a decadent richness that complements the candied pumpkin perfectly.*

   Tip: Use a potato peeler to peel the orange.

INGREDIENTS

Pumpkin
1 (2 1/2-pound) pie pumpkin
4 cups water
4 (8-ounce) piloncillo cones
1 (3-inch-long) strip of orange peel
3 Mexican cinnamon sticks
1/4 teaspoon ground ginger
2 whole cloves
1 star anise

Toppings
syrup
milk or heavy whipping cream

Ponche Navideño

My *niña* Diana taught me how to make *ponche*. It was at her house I had it for the first time and fell in love. This hot, fruity, sweet Christmas punch is typically served during *Posadas* (a religious Christmas festival) and on Christmas Eve. I serve it throughout the entire month of December and usually spike it with tequila for festivities. When tequila is added, it goes from being *ponche navideño* (Christmas punch) to *ponche con piquete* (spiked or "picket" punch). Both ways of serving are equally special—just depends on the company.

Prep Time: 15 minutes   *Cook Time: 3 hours*   *Yield: 25 to 30 cups (enough for a small party)*

1. Place all ingredients in a large pot over high heat and bring to a boil.
2. When the mixture starts to boil and the piloncillo cones have melted, reduce heat to low. Cover with a lid and cook for 3 hours.
3. Remove from heat and serve hot.

   Tip: You can use any kind of apple. I use a red apple.

   Tip: Add a shot of tequila to your cup to bring on the con piquete.

INGREDIENTS

2 gallons water
15 tamarind pods, peeled and deveined
18 dried hibiscus flowers
4 Mexican cinnamon sticks
20 tejocote (hawthorn)
5 apples, cut in half and cored, or 10 whole crimson gold apples
2 *membrillo* (quince) fruits, cored and cut into pieces
15 guavas
1/2 cup raisins
20 prunes, pitted
8 ounces sugarcane
3 (8-ounce) piloncillo cones

Buñuelos (Fritters)

These fried fritters are prepared year-round, but they accentuate the holiday season and are especially tasty served with a cup of *chocolate caliente!* The trick to these *buñuelos* is to roll them as paper-thin as possible and let them dry out slightly before frying.

Prep Time: 30 minutes   Rest Time: 30 minutes   Cook Time: 30 minutes   Yield: 12 buñuelos

DOUGH

1. To prepare cinnamon tea, in a saucepan bring water and cinnamon sticks to a boil, then remove from heat and steep for 10 minutes. Remove cinnamon stick.
2. In a stand mixer fitted with the dough attachment, add flour, sugar, baking powder, and salt. Mix to combine.
3. Add warm cinnamon tea, vegetable oil, and orange extract. Mix for a few minutes until dough has formed a ball and is no longer sticky. If dough is still sticky, add flour a tablespoon at a time until dough is no longer sticky.
4. Remove dough from mixer and place on a floured work surface. Knead with hands for 2 to 3 minutes, adding flour until dough is no longer sticky and is very soft.
5. Cover dough with a small bowl and allow to rest for 30 minutes.
6. Cut dough into 12 equal pieces. Roll each piece into a ball. Cover with a towel and allow to rest for a few minutes.
7. Dip balls of dough in some flour, then roll out with rolling pin until dough is paper-thin. Set to the side.

FRYING

1. Mix sugar and cinnamon on a plate. Line another plate with paper towels. Set to the side.
2. In a heavy-bottomed pot with a candy thermometer attached to the side, add 2 inches oil and heat to 350 degrees. Place dough in oil and cook until dough is golden crisp, about 1 minute on each side.
3. Drain each *buñuelo* on prepared plate. Dip in cinnamon sugar and serve.

INGREDIENTS

vegetable oil for frying

Dough
3/4 cup water
1 Mexican cinnamon stick
2 cups plus 2 tablespoons flour
1 1/2 tablespoons sugar
1 1/2 teaspoons baking powder
1/2 teaspoon salt
3 tablespoons vegetable oil
1/2 teaspoon orange extract

Cinnamon Sugar
1/2 cup sugar
1 tablespoon ground cinnamon

Buñuelos de Viento (Light-as-the-Wind Fritters)

Light as air, *Buñuelos de Viento* are crispy, crunchy happiness. They are mostly enjoyed during the holiday season. I can't imagine *Posadas* or Christmas without them. Their delicate blow-in-the-wind shape is beautifully decorative; they look like they belong on center stage. To make these, you will need a rosette iron, also known as a *buñuelera*.

Prep Time: 10 minutes   *Rest Time: 20 minutes*   *Cook Time: 20 minutes*   *Yield: 10 servings*

DOUGH

1. Whisk eggs, melted butter, and sugar together. Add milk and vanilla and whisk to combine completely.
2. In a separate bowl mix flour, baking powder, and salt together. Sift dry ingredients into wet ingredients. Whisk to combine. Mixture should have the consistency of thick cream.
3. Allow batter to rest for 20 minutes.

FRYING

1. Mix sugar and cinnamon on a plate. Line another plate with paper towels. Set to the side.
2. Fill a small frying pan fitted with a candy thermometer with 2 inches oil. Place pan over medium heat and allow to reach 325 degrees.
3. Dip rosette iron into hot oil, allowing it to get hot, then remove it and blot off excess oil. Dip rosette into batter, making sure to leave the top of the rosette exposed. Do not submerge it all the way. Dip rosette with batter back into hot oil. Fry for about 20 seconds. The *buñuelo* will easily slip off. Once the *buñuelo* slips off, place rosette to the side. Use tongs to flip the *buñuelo* over and cook it on the inside. Let fry until golden crisp, another 40 seconds. Repeat with remaining batter.
4. Drain each *buñuelo* on prepared plate. Dip in cinnamon sugar and serve.

INGREDIENTS

vegetable oil for frying

Dough
2 eggs
1 tablespoon butter, melted and cooled
2 tablespoons sugar
1 cup milk
1 teaspoon Mexican vanilla extract
1 cup flour
1 1/2 teaspoons baking powder
1/8 teaspoon salt

Cinnamon Sugar
1/2 cup sugar
1 tablespoon ground cinnamon

Rosca de Reyes (Three Kings' Cake)

This bread is eaten in the days leading up to Three Kings' Day. Typically children in Latin America and Spain celebrate the three kings on January 6, which marks the end of the twelve days of Christmas. It is believed that three kings came on the twelfth day by guidance of the North Star and found baby Jesus along with his parents in Bethlehem. The kings bestowed gifts on the newborn king, and during the celebration of Three Kings' Day, gifts are exchanged and a serious celebration is had by all.

One way people celebrate is by making *rosca de reyes*, which has little toy babies baked inside. Enjoying the *rosca* becomes a big event where a group of people gather to eat it, and if your slice has a toy baby in it, then you are appointed to provide a *tamal* dinner for everyone on February 2 for *Día de la Candelaria*.

Prep Time: *30 minutes*   **Rest Time:** *3 hours*   **Bake Time:** *25 minutes*   **Yield:** *2 roscas*

DOUGH

1. In a small bowl combine yeast, 1 tablespoon sugar, and warm milk. Mix to combine and allow to get frothy, about 10 minutes.
2. In a stand mixer fitted with the whisk attachment, whisk remaining 1 cup sugar, flour, and salt together. Change the attachment to a dough hook and add butter. Mix on medium-low speed until butter is incorporated and forms pea-sized balls, about 3 minutes. Stop the mixer and scrape down flour into center periodically.
3. Add eggs, vanilla, and orange extract. Mix until fully incorporated, stopping the mixer periodically to run a rubber spatula along the bottom to bring up any flour.
4. Add activated yeast. Mix with dough hook on medium for about 10 minutes. Dough will be soft and a bit sticky.
5. Remove dough from mixer and place on a floured surface. Knead for 1 or 2 minutes, adding small amounts of flour as you knead until dough comes together easily and is no longer sticky.
6. Shape dough into a ball. Place in greased bowl, cover with plastic wrap, and set in a warm place (80 to 85 degrees). Let dough double in size for 2 hours.

INGREDIENTS

Dough
1 1/2 tablespoons active dry yeast
1 cup plus 1 tablespoon sugar, divided
2/3 cup milk, warm (between 100 and 110 degrees)
6 cups flour
1/2 tablespoon salt
1 cup butter, room temperature
6 eggs
1 teaspoon Mexican vanilla extract
1 teaspoon orange extract
6 little plastic baby dolls

Rosca Pasta
1/2 cup butter
1 cup flour
3/4 cup confectioners' sugar
1 egg yolk
gel food coloring (optional)

Egg Wash
1 egg
1 tablespoon water

Toppings
ate de membrillo (quince paste)
dried candied figs
2 tablespoons sugar

7. Line two baking sheets with nonstick baking mats. Set to the side.
8. Divide dough in half. Place one half on a floured work surface and roll into a 9x13-inch rectangle. Roll dough into a tight log, distributing 3 baby dolls throughout the dough halfway. Bring the ends of the dough together to form an oval-shaped ring. Place on prepared baking sheet with the seam underneath. Repeat with remaining dough.

ROSCA PASTA

1. In a stand mixer fitted with the paddle attachment, mix butter and flour together. Add confectioners' sugar and mix until fully combined. Add egg yolk and mix for another minute or until mixture comes together easily. If the mixture is too wet and does not resemble paste, add an additional tablespoon flour. If you decide to color the *rosca pasta*, add 1 to 2 drops of gel coloring and mix to combine.
2. Place on a floured surface. Roll out with a rolling pin to a 1/8-inch thickness. Cut into thick strips and various star shapes.

ASSEMBLY

1. To prepare egg wash, whisk egg and water together. Using a pastry brush, brush the top of the rosca dough with egg wash.
2. Decorate the top of the rosca dough with *rosca pasta, membrillo* fruit paste, and dried candied figs. Sprinkle with sugar.
3. Allow to rise for 1 hour or until doubled in size.
4. Heat oven to 350 degrees. Bake for 25 minutes.

Bebidas
(Drinks)

Cinnamon *Atole*

This creamy, warm Aztecan beverage is perfectly sweet and slightly thick with just the right amount of cinnamon. It is mild in flavor and serves as the ideal partner to many desserts during colder weather.

Prep Time: 5 minutes   *Cook Time: 15 minutes*   *Yield: 4 cups*

1. In a bowl mix cornstarch and 1/4 cup cold water until cornstarch dissolves. Set to the side.
2. In a saucepan over medium heat, add remaining 2 cups water, cinnamon sticks, and piloncillo. Cook for 15 minutes to melt piloncillo and perfume the water with cinnamon.
3. Pour cinnamon-water mixture into a blender. Blend until smooth, then pour through a sieve to collect all cinnamon particles. Discard particles.
4. Return cinnamon water to saucepan. Add milk, vanilla, and salt. Cook over medium heat, stirring constantly so milk doesn't burn, until mixture comes to a boil.
5. Add cornstarch mixture and mix until thickened. Enjoy warm.

INGREDIENTS

2 1/2 tablespoons cornstarch
2 1/4 cups water, divided
5 Mexican cinnamon sticks
1 (8-ounce) piloncillo cone
4 cups milk
1/2 teaspoon Mexican vanilla extract
pinch of salt

Café de Olla

This beverage is a caffeinated delicacy to be savored and served any time of the day. *Café de olla* is unlike a regular cup of joe, as it is spiced with sweet hints of cinnamon, clove, and orange. No *abuelita* or *abuelito* would ever turn it away, and all the *tías* will be asking for your recipe.

Prep Time: 3 minutes   *Cook Time: 15 minutes*   *Steep Time: 10 minutes*   *Yield: 6 cups*

1. Add all ingredients except coffee grounds to a pot over medium heat. Mix until piloncillo dissolves and water comes to a boil, about 15 minutes.
2. Slowly sprinkle coffee over boiling water and mix to combine. Remove from heat and allow coffee to steep for 7 to 10 minutes.
3. Strain mixture through a fine mesh sieve lined with cheesecloth. Discard particles.
4. Serve and enjoy.

Tip: To enhance the flavor further, I use 100% arabica cinnamon-flavored medium roast coffee grounds.

INGREDIENTS

4 ounces piloncillo
6 cups water
1 Mexican cinnamon stick
1 teaspoon Mexican vanilla extract
2 whole cloves
3 raw almonds
2 (3-inch-long) pieces orange peel
6 tablespoons coffee grounds

Chocolate Caliente de Agua

I learned to make this version of *chocolate caliente* from my husband's ninety-five-year-old grandmother, who lives in Mexicali, BC. *Chocolate de agua* is made with a water base instead of milk and allows the chocolate flavor to shine through as the main star.

Prep Time: 25 minutes   *Yield: 8 cups*

1. Add water, cinnamon sticks, and vanilla to a small pot over medium-high heat. Bring water to a boil. Once water is at a rolling boil, remove cinnamon sticks.
2. Add chocolate to boiling water. Allow chocolate to fully melt, then pour in evaporated milk. Mix to combine. Use a molinillo to help break up chocolate by twisting it back and forth between the palms of your hands.
3. Serve and enjoy.

INGREDIENTS

8 cups water
2 Mexican cinnamon sticks
1 teaspoon Mexican vanilla extract
4 disks Mexican chocolate
1 (12-ounce) can evaporated milk

My Deepest Gratitude

Thank you to my lifelong partner, Mando, for supporting me in all my food endeavors and for jumping on board as my photographer for this book. You made my food visions come to life. My world goes round with you in it, and I am forever grateful for your fierce devotion to our family and the dedicated love you show me daily. I love you, Ugly Bear, and am lucky to have you.

Thank you to my only child, Max, for being such a sweet and happy boy. You make motherhood a joy, and I can't imagine my universe without you in it. Please continue to smile big, and keep the curiosity and zest for life in your eyes. I love you on a grand scale, my beautiful boy.

Thank you to my mom for loving me unconditionally and guiding me through life. I can't imagine how hard it must have been for you to raise me as a single mother. I love you so much and cherish our unbreakable bond for eternity.

Thank you to my auntie Rosie, my second mom who helped raise me, who let me get my hands dirty in her kitchen as a child and still to this day. I will keep your cooking tips deep in my soul every time I'm in the kitchen. I love you, *Tía*.

Thank you to my auntie Hope for letting me be bossy and bratty in your kitchen as I sharpened my baking skills. *Gracias* for putting up with all the cakes I used to bake for us in Los Feliz and beyond. And many thanks for taking me to far-off places around the world and accompanying me to all the bakeries along the way. Love always to my *Brilla preciosa*!

Thank you to my uncle Ron for teaching me how to make life sparkle. You and I were poor kids from City Terrace who knew how to live. I said it once before, and I'll say it again: I feel like I can walk on the moon when I'm with you.

Thank you to my entire Sandoval family and all my beautiful cousins for loving me, protecting me as a child, and always welcoming my desserts and dishes to our family gatherings.

Thank you to my Presley family for helping shape my palate at a young age. Thank you for supporting me and encouraging me with words of praise and by serving yourselves seconds.

Thank you to my Lopez/Caldera/Flores family for welcoming me with open arms. It's been a privilege cooking for you since day one. I love you all.

To my chosen Hermana-Hood:

Ericka—Thank you for driving me to take the leap into the book world. You know I would have never done this without your nudge, and this is just the beginning for us. Thank you for being my food partner and more importantly one of my dearest friends. Love you, *amiga*. <3

Marisela—Thank you for being the epitome of a true friend. I love that our friendship continues to flourish and grow. May it live for another three lifetimes. <3

Tonantzin—Thank you for being the glue behind our monthly *amiga* dinners. It is a gift to have you in my life, and cheers to many more years of being here for one another.

Monica, Angie, Lou—Thank you for adopting me into your tight circle. I love our profound conversations and am so inspired by all that you ladies do for the city of Los Angeles. *Pandemic Pansas por Vida!*

Gicel—Thank you for being one of my favorite people on the planet. No subject is off-limits. I love seeing you happy and being your true self. <3 Shine bright.

Lucy—Thank you for the many moons of friendship. I love that we always reconnect no matter how busy we become. Thank you, Lady Gallardo, for capturing that moment in Berkeley and allowing me to use the photo for this book. You're a treasured gem.

A-dre—I'm glad you decided to get in the car with the crazy chicken. Ha! Thank you, Adriana, for being a loyal friend and for dealing with me asking you for your opinions during the making of this book. You rock, girlfriend.

Monique—Thank you for your unwavering support and for being a constant cheerleader of mine. You are the sweetest girl on the planet, and everyone deserves to have a friend like you, Mo.

Tony Molina—Thank you for always believing in everything I do in the food world, and for all your help and support throughout the years. I'm forever grateful.

Thank you to all my friends for putting up with my endless food talk and living life with me as confidants! Kathy, Yolanda, Rachel, Stephen, Art, Isa, Nancy, and my sweet *ratita* Natalia!

Thank you to Melissa's Produce for your support and to MyCajita for providing props for my *Pan de Muertos* photo.

Thank you to my Familius family: The real-life Christopher Robbins, Ashley Mireles, Ashlin Awerkamp, Carlos Guerrero, and Brooke Jorden! Thank you for welcoming me into your exclusive book club. I feel honored to be a part of the Familius publishing house library. Cheers to our first book together. Until the next one!

About the Author

Born and raised in Los Angeles's eastside, **Nicole Presley** is a Latina culinary enthusiast and recipe developer passionate about her culture and food. She is self-taught and inspired to keep the traditional Mexican desserts of her childhood alive with her recipes. She is also a master of Mexican-American fusion desserts to honor her duel cultures and take your taste buds on a magnificent culinary journey. Nicole uses her skills that combine cooking and beautiful food art to create accessible recipes for thousands of followers on her social media platforms, known as Presley's Pantry. She has been hired by some of the country's most renowned companies as a food stylist and recipe developer, and has landed her some of the most incredible experiences that continue to shape her footprint in the culinary world. In her first book, Nicole uses her personal and professional experiences to create decadent desserts from her East LA kitchen that pay homage to her roots and celebrate all the sweetness life has to offer.

Nicole lives in East Los Angeles with her husband, her thirteen-year-old son, and her two chihuahuas.

About Familius

VISIT OUR WEBSITE: WWW.FAMILIUS.COM

Familius is a global trade publishing company that publishes books and other content to help families be happy. We believe that the family is the fundamental unit of society and that happy families are the foundation of a happy life. We recognize that every family looks different, and we passionately believe in helping all families find greater joy. To that end, we publish books for children and adults that invite families to live the Familius Ten Habits of Happy Family Life: **love together, play together, learn together, work together, talk together, heal together, read together, eat together, give together**, and **laugh together**. Founded in 2012, Familius is located in Sanger, California.

CONNECT

Facebook: www.facebook.com/familiustalk

Twitter: @familiustalk, @paterfamilius1

Pinterest: www.pinterest.com/familius

Instagram: @familiustalk

The most important work you ever do will be within the walls of your own home.